THE TAKE GOOD CARE OF
MY SON
Cookbook
for Brides

THE TAKE GOOD CARE OF
MY SON
Cookbook
for Brides

BY
June Roth

AN ESSANDESS SPECIAL EDITION

NEW YORK

The charts and photographs
which appear on pages 61–69 and 70–75
are reproduced through the courtesy of
the National Livestock and Meat Board, Chicago, Illinois.

THE TAKE GOOD CARE OF MY SON
COOKBOOK FOR BRIDES

SBN: 671-10372-5

With
loving thoughts
of my son
Bob

Foreword

CONGRATULATIONS! YOU ARE ABOUT TO—OR HAVE JUST—MARried a mother's son. I hope his mother reared your man on a balanced formula of warm devotion and wholesome neglect. Now it is your turn to be the number one female in his life and to assume the responsibility for his nutritional well-being.

In fairy tales, the prince finally marries the princess, they live happily ever after, and the story fades out . . . "The End." In truth, it is "The Beginning" and the time when you may most appreciate a book which is designed to help you adjust to your new role as a homemaker.

Don't expect me to tell you how to boil water and how to crack an egg—other books have been written which do that job quite well. My goal is to inspire you to take such pride in your new status that you will want to put a great deal of effort into the early learning years. I am going to tell you what your mother may have forgotten to say, and what your mother-in-law might not dare to say. And then I am going to share with you many culinary tricks and shortcuts that will make you a knowledgeable cook.

We may never meet, but you will soon realize that I am deeply concerned about your attitude toward the job you have undertaken, and your success in strengthening your marriage.

My words at times may sound old-fashioned—I hope they do—
for my latest coiffure and newest fashions are only this year's
wrappings for an old-fashioned viewpoint which I value dearly.
This book has been brewing in my mind for several years. I
wanted to write it while I was young enough to remember and
yet old enough to give advice from years of experience. I want
to help you, if you will let me.

Marriage is like a pot of stew: If you measure too carefully
what you put into it, it is apt to be thin and stingy, but if you
heap it full of unmeasured effort, it will be hearty and satisfying
to those who share its bounty.

I wish for you the willingness to learn, the courage to be
adventurous in the kitchen, and the comfort of a man who loves
you and appreciates your efforts.

Most sincerely,
JUNE ROTH

Contents

1

On Being a Wife

WHAT IS SO GREAT ABOUT LEARNING TO COOK?

Everything!

You become adept instead of inept.

You conquer and control the nerve-tranquilizing center of your home. You give to the man you love and to your progeny a bonus for life, while releasing and developing creative talents that will keep you interesting and good-humored the rest of your days. T.V. dinners were intended as emergency fare, not as a way of life for a loving wife!

Always remember that it is the woman who establishes the emotional climate of the home. Her positive attitude toward cooking and her proud estimate of the value of her job as a homemaker will be reflected in the happiness and contentment of her family.

Just as your destiny is tied to your husband's ability and ambition, so the fulfillment of his desire for a cheerful, well-managed household is linked to your attitude about your home. You are going to be a *can-do-it-girl* or a *can't-do-it-girl*. Your housekeeping decisions may be made in piecemeal order, but in a short time they will reveal the pattern of your future years together.

If you are used to bragging with an air of charming helplessness that you can't even boil water, look to the years ahead and realize that your indifference will produce roughly a thousand boring meals a year. Let's hope you successfully reach your golden wedding anniversary without the curse of fifty thousand dreary dining dilemmas!

Now—right now—is the time to make the decision, regardless of whether your mother or mother-in-law is an imaginative or an indifferent homemaker. You, as a young bride embarking on your own unique adventure in married life, have the right to chart your course with creative intelligence. Don't expect perfection in the beginning, but do acquire a willingness to learn the basic skills and to use them.

While you should not expect your bridegroom to achieve immediately the financial security which took your father over twenty years to reach, so, too, he should be realistic about the quality of your homemaking skills, when compared to his mother's practiced hands. Each spouse should exhibit patience and encouragement when evaluating the other's performance. Constant growth is the best criterion during the learning years that set the stage for the years of teamwork ahead.

Common sense, for example, will tell you that if your husband is a meat and potatoes man he will not appreciate a menu of creamed dishes, casseroles, and wine cookery night after night. However, this does not mean that you should limit your skills to the simple foods he is used to. Try your hand at new dishes but with ample time spaced between the new foods so that the entire menu formula does not change dramatically overnight.

In like manner, when cooking for company concentrate on the few dishes you do extremely well rather than experimenting with a completely new group of preparations. It might be a good idea to prepare one new dessert or side dish each time until you become accustomed to producing company dinners with ease. Conquer company-dinner panic early in your career, or it will throw you into a tailspin forever after.

I know one young couple, who during their first year of marriage, arranged a weekly bowling date with another newlywed pair. The plan was to begin the evening by dining alternately at each other's home, and then to spend the rest of the evening bowling. Somehow the dinners became a challenge for the new cooks. Their unspoken pact not to repeat the same menu during the year encouraged each young bride to become an imaginative cook. Both young women consider that year of experimental cooking as the inspiration for the fine dining they have enjoyed ever since.

Life is like a kaleidoscope, changing its patterns every day and requiring great adaptability to cope with the many roles a woman must play. In addition to being a general jack-of-all-homemaking skills, she must have an artistic sense when dealing with food. Consider the importance of color, texture, and form when planning your meals and be sure that you provide a varied menu that is pleasing to the eye as well as to the palate. A creamed fish dish served with cauliflower, mashed potatoes, and stewed pears on the side would be a dull offering. Not only would the colors be similar, but all the textures would be soft and all the flavors bland. Designing an eye-appealing menu is a skill that demands planning and good taste.

You are lucky to be learning to cook at a time when food manufacturers are vying with each other to produce an endless assortment of convenience foods, frozen foods, and packaged foods, to make your job easier and less time-consuming. You can pick and choose the special products that will best serve your needs. Your choice should be based on economy—both time and money. Many modern products will save both; some will save time but cost far more money than the duplicate homemade product, and you will have to decide whether the time saved merits the extra expense. Sometimes it does and sometimes it doesn't, and I intend to introduce you to a large number of dependable convenience products that will earn your approval as well as give you a basis for making judgments about other products.

In general, convenience products will help you to cultivate an adventurous attitude in the kitchen and allow you to use shortcuts to achieve old-fashioned tastes. They will help you to achieve a varied menu without having to slave over a hot stove for hours. They will inspire you to be economy-minded without the feeling that you are producing inferior-quality meals. Above all, they will open to you a boundless horizon of creative cooking that will transform your thousand meals a year into satisfying dining—not feeding—sessions.

✢ 2 ✢

Decisions! Decisions!

EFFICIENCY IS HABIT-FORMING. SO IS CARELESSNESS! ONE HABIT is acquired by deliberate perseverance; the other will sneak up on you if you don't care enough. It is all a matter of practice, and you must decide early in your marriage which habit will bring you the most return for your efforts.

There are people who are habitually late, habitually messy, who clutter up their lives with half-finished projects. They always spend precious time apologizing for their carelessness. While helplessness may be an appealing trait during courtship it may turn out to be unendurable over a lifetime. At the other extreme are the nervous wrecks who make a fetish out of orderliness and who hover over their guests until they suffocate any breath of relaxed pleasure in their presence. This extremism starts as a habit too and can become a curse!

What should be the ideal goal, then? First, to create a relaxed home atmosphere; second, to acquire a sense of tidiness as you work. My main concern is how you function in the kitchen, but in truth those work habits are a reflection of your other house-keeping and personal habits. The teenage sloppy rebellion period can carry over a lifetime, if you allow it to.

Arrange your kitchen equipment with an eye to saving time and motion as you use each item. Keep the decks clear at all

4

times. Don't let dishes pile up. A squirt of detergent in a basin of hot water will be a standing invitation to each utensil as you finish using it. If you need it again, rinse it, use it, and dunk it some more. Ditto with dishes and glasses. Soak them and let the detergent do the dirty work while you keep the decks clear. Rinse and drain all items while you wipe around the stove and sweep the floor. Dry off the remaining drops and put everything away. *Put everything away* is the key phrase if you want to develop the habit of orderliness. It is the cornerstone of speed in the kitchen.

One way you can show affection for your husband is to care about what he is coming home to. Don't bother with household sprays that remove the aromas of good cooking. A man should have the pleasure of sniffing his way from the front door to the kitchen, following the promise of something delicious being made just for him. Marriage counselors would do well to advise the young bride to slice half an onion and simmer it gently in a bit of butter a few minutes before the groom comes home. Throw the onion out if you have to, but only after the delicious aroma has shouted, "Welcome home!"

If you set the table before you start preparing dinner, you are more likely to take the time to make it attractive. Those dinners for two before you were married required a pretty table cloth, some thought about the dishes and glassware, and a great deal of thought about the menu. Well, now that you've got your man, make sure that that sample of your domesticity was a reliable example of meals to come. Plastic plates belong at a picnic, and dinner-for-two deserves some of your nicer things . . . not your best china and linen, perhaps, but certainly something attractive. Use a surprise serving dish now and then. Don't let things get dull, in the kitchen or anywhere else.

The challenge of everyday food preparation becomes child's play when compared to the challenge of the company dinner. Always remember that the first item on the menu should be a relaxed hostess. That's you!

What makes for a relaxed hostess? Planning! You'll have a sense of great security and peace of mind when the behind-the-scenes operations have been so well planned that your job as hostess seems effortless. There is no better guarantee for a successful dinner party than a hostess who has planned her work and then casually worked her plan.

Your guests will probably remember the atmosphere of your home long after they have forgotten the menu. To keep things cheerful and free of pressure, plan a menu that will wait without spoiling and one that permits all or most of the cooking to be done in advance.

A good working procedure is to make a list of all the foods you want to serve, checking for variety of colors and textures, and then for compatability of tastes. Next, consider the time schedule your menu requires. Will the oven be free for heating those hors d'oeuvres and rolls, or would cold canapés with cocktails relieve some of the pressure? Changing the menu at the planning stage is easier than fiddling with the pots and oven while your guests burn!

This is also the time to select the one special dish that will make your dinner memorable. Don't overextend yourself by planning an entire menu of complicated specialties, but do arrange to include one dish in your main course that is not the same old thing that everyone else serves. For company cooking, your dessert should always look beautiful, taste delicious, and be served with style. Why not? It is not much more difficult to prepare something lovely, and the pride and satisfaction you experience will make the effort worthwhile.

The "voice of virtue" rarely speaks above a whisper these days, but for those who choose to tune in, life can be sweet. If you show the man you love, and whose name you share and whose social image you represent, that you *care*, he will surely bask in the compliments you both receive. He chose you above all others, to love and to cherish from that wedding day forward. Every thoughtful thing you do will remind him of how wise he was, and what a clever fellow he continues to be. Besides loving each other, it is delightful to "like" your marriage partner. The decisions you make today can be the foundation for a lifetime of admiration from the man you married.

Remember that you can learn as much from mistakes as you can from success—so get into the habit of making decisions and revising them accordingly.

❧ 3 ❧

Home Engineering

How can you handle unexpected company without resorting to a hot tuna fish casserole? A clever girl I know, whose husband has a position that necessitates bringing home a surprise dinner guest occasionally, has met this problem with good humor and imagination. She cannot refuse to cooperate without jeopardizing her husband's career, and a poor dinner would do little for his prestige. Facing matters squarely, she works out one elegant emergency dinner menu each year. It must go from the freezer to the table in one hour, and it must be a conversation piece. When used, the entire menu is immediately replaced the next day.

One year the menu consisted of two roasted chickens, frozen in white wine–mushroom gravy and served on a bed of green noodles with candied whole carrots on the side. The first course was eggs à la russe garnished with capers. Dessert was a hot fruit compote simmered in red wine with a dash of cinnamon added to the fruit syrups, and served with fancy cookies.

Analyzing this menu, for those who have no freezer, the emergency shopping list includes:

> 2 jars of large chicken slices
> 1 can sliced mushrooms
> 1 can consomme

7

1 pound green noodles
1 can whole tiny carrots
1 jar of capers
1 can peach halves
1 can pear halves
1 can apricot halves
1 pound assorted cookies

From your everyday provisions you would use eggs for boiling, chili sauce and mayonnaise mixed together to make the Russian dressing, brown sugar and butter to candy the carrots, white and red domestic wines, dried onions, Gravy Master, cinnamon, flour, and lemon juice.

Here is the way that dinner, serving four, is prepared:

1. Hard-boil 4 eggs, shell them, and cut in half lengthwise. Whisk ½ cup mayonnaise into ½ cup chili sauce. Arrange 2 halves of egg on each small plate, spoon the Russian dressing over them, letting some of the egg show, and garnish with capers. Dash some paprika over the top. Refrigerate. (See Eggs à la Russe, page 163.)

2. While the eggs are boiling, put up water to boil for the noodles.

3. In a third pot, empty the can of consomme (undiluted), mushrooms, 2 tablespoons dried onion flakes, 2 tablespoons Gravy Master, ½ cup white wine, and 2 tablespoons lemon juice. Simmer. Then thicken slightly with 2 tablespoons flour, mixed first with a little cold water to prevent lumping. Stir while the gravy is thickening. (See White Wine–Mushroom Gravy, page 133.)

4. Empty carrots into a small saucepan, pouring off most of the juice. Add a bouillon cube, and heat until dissolved. Add 2 tablespoons butter and 2 tablespoons of brown sugar. Simmer and stir until evenly coated. (See Elegant Carrots, pages 103–04.)

5. Drop the noodles into boiling water for 10 minutes. Drain. Arrange canned chicken pieces over the noodles and top with the hot white wine gravy. Place in a 200-degree oven until ready to serve within the hour.

6. Rinse out the noodle pot and combine canned fruits in it. Add ½ teaspoon cinnamon, 1 tablespoon lemon juice, and ½ cup red wine. Simmer for 5 minutes. Serve des-

8

sert at the table from a large fancy bowl into individual fruit dishes. (See Hot Fruit Compote, page 150.)

A slowpoke could prepare this meal in a half hour. The smart cook would have preceded the schedule by reaching for a box of blueberry muffin mix and baking the mixture in a one-quart fluted aluminum gelatin mold. By the time you turn the oven to 200 degrees for the chicken–noodle dish, you would have a giant muffin-shaped tea bread, freshly baked and just waiting for a slathering of soft butter.

Now set the table with your best things. Light the candles, place the homemade bread on a pretty dish or board to serve as your centerpiece, and enjoy the dinner with your guests. Accept the compliments graciously; only you will know the ease with which the emergency was met and conquered.

An alternate menu might be: hot crab meat on herbed croutons, steak with Burgundy–mushroom gravy, wild and white rice, green beans amandine, and blueberry parfaits. A giant cornbread muffin would be your centerpiece.

Your marketing list includes:

2 cans crab meat
1 package croutons
1 large thick steak
1 can sliced mushrooms
2 cans (or frozen) French-style green beans
1 can slivered almonds
1 package Uncle Ben's White and Wild Rice
1 can blueberry pie filling
1 quart vanilla ice cream
1 package corn muffin mix

Your procedure would be:

1. Mix and pop the corn muffin mix into the oven.
2. Follow package directions for the rice dish.
3. Empty mushrooms with liquid into a saucepan, add ½ cup Burgundy wine, 2 tablespoons dried onions, 2 tablespoons dried parsley, 2 teaspoons Gravy Master, and 1 cup water. Simmer for 5 minutes. Thicken with 2 tablespoons flour as in the chicken gravy. (See Burgundy–Mushroom Gravy, page 132.)
4. Heat the beans, drain, add 2 tablespoons butter, and

serve with a sprinkling of canned slivered almonds. (See Green Beans Amandine, page 102.)

5. Broil steak 20 minutes before serving. Slice at table and serve smothered in Burgundy–Mushroom Gravy.

While the steak is broiling:

6. Heat a skillet; add ½ cup olive oil or other cooking oil, 2 tablespoons onion flakes, 2 tablespoons dried parsley, and 2 cloves of peeled crushed garlic (use a garlic press). Break canned crab meat into bite-sized pieces. Sauté gently, turning pieces to coat with onion, parsley, and garlic. Serve on herbed croutons or on toast points. (See Hot Crab Meat on Herbed Croutons, page 56.)

7. Make parfaits by alternating vanilla ice cream with spoonfuls of blueberry pie filling.

Keeping these shortcuts in mind, I am going to give you a list of staples to keep on hand always. They will help to transform your ordinary cooking efforts into gourmet offerings.

❧ 4 ❧

Don't Play House

THE VARIETY OF EQUIPMENT YOU NEED TO BUY WILL DEPEND ON the scope of your cooking ambitions. You cannot hope to assemble every item immediately, but as you buy each new pot and pan, make sure that it is a top-quality item. You may think that any cheap substitute will do, but experience will teach you that temporary possessions have a way of becoming permanent.

Be ruthless about exchanging frivolous gifts for practical, good-quality necessities, unless the toes you step on will cause a reverberating ache for years to come. A few pretty casseroles are all right, but don't expect to be able to do top-of-the-stove cooking with them unless you are prepared to hover like a hawk over scorchable cookware. Stainless steel pots that are too thin will provoke a sailorlike vocabulary, and cheaply lined Teflon products will be useless after the first scratchings. Beauty is truly in the eye of the beholder, and heavy-duty aluminum cookware will seem absolutely gorgeous after you have had some bad experiences with powder-puff products.

For aluminum baking pans, buy the shiniest heaviest quality you can afford. Supermarkets will offer inexpensive, dull, or seamed pans and you may wonder why you should pay more for the same-sized product that will do the same job. The "bargain" pans will get duller and harder to clean after several usings; the

11

good-quality pans will be feeding your grandchildren.

Don't be gadget-happy and buy impractical tools that will only collect dust over the years. Make sure that each time-saving implement will do just that—not add to the clutter of things that have a way of taking up space in your kitchen drawers. A good rubber scraper, for example, will save ounces of batter from every bowl; a good peeler will prevent wasteful motions and thick peels; a curved grapefruit knife will pave the way to graceful scooping at the table; a good food chopper will make quick work of that chore; and a heavy-duty quality wire whisk will guarantee a smooth product every time.

The one item you may economize on is fancy molds for gelatin desserts. There are pretty copper-colored molds made of tin on the market which are much less expensive than the solid copper collectors' items; and they will do the same job. However, if you plan to use the mold for tea-bread baking as well as for fancy desserts of gelatin, buy the aluminum variety.

A small electric hand mixer is adequate for simple jobs, but it is a toy when it comes to beating a cake batter. Keep one if it is a gift, but do invest in a good regular-sized mixer as soon as you can. Some mixers come with many attachments, and some lift off the stand and can be used as a portable mixer. Shop around and compare brands, examining the attachments carefully to evaluate if each attachment is sturdy enough to do the promised job. This appliance can be your extra right arm for many years, if you choose wisely.

A good set of knives can also last a lifetime. Keep them sharpened, but have a healthy respect for their potential danger. Don't throw them carelessly into a drawer. This will ruin the blades and cause you to slice a finger now and then as you grope for the right knife. A knife rack placed in a drawer or hung on a wall is a safety measure for you and your equipment.

A well-organized kitchen must be logically planned. Before you rush to put things away in the approximate places they occupied in your mother's kitchen, analyze your own available space. The larger the kitchen the more thought you must give to avoiding waste motion—preventing two or three steps for something that could be accomplished in one reach. At times this may necessitate having duplicate equipment in key spots: two sets of hanging measuring cups and spoons, or two sets of hanging kitchen utensils. A little forethought will save you time and energy.

In the long run, the quality of your kitchen equipment will affect your cooking skills. Be sure that the tools you use will not impede your ability to be a superb cook!

STAPLE LIST FOR GOURMET COOKING

White wine
Burgundy wine
Sherry wine
Concentrated lemon juice
Dried onion flakes
Dried parsley flakes
Head of garlic
Bay leaves
Basil
Grated lemon peel
Paprika
Onion soup mix
Wild rice/white rice
Muffin mixes
Dried potatoes (mashed)
Canned condensed
  cream of mushroom soup
Grated Parmesan cheese
Brown sugar
Canned crab meat
Canned mushrooms
Canned French fried onions
Blueberry pie filling
Cherry pie filling

Buy small sizes of domestic white, Burgundy, and sherry wines with screw-on caps. Use the white wine in sauces for chicken, turkey, and fish; the Burgundy wine to splash over roast beef, to add to beef gravies, pot roasts, and stews; the sherry wine to pep up cream soups, cream sauces, and some chicken dishes. The alcohol evaporates after a few moments of cooking but the flavor lingers on. California and New York wines are good for cooking. Be sure to replace the caps immediately after using and refrigerate once a bottle has been opened. Gallo-brand wines are also good and they keep exceptionally well. Experiment until you find the brand that you prefer and then use it.

Concentrated lemon juice is a must unless you intend to keep fresh lemons in the refrigerator at all times. Use a tablespoon or so in the water in which you boil shrimp; add a teaspoon to a plain cake mix; add lemon juice to melted butter for a lobster dip; sprinkle it over fish and poultry for happier tastes; add it with sugar to most tomato based dishes; add a teaspoonful to a lemon pie mix for a homemade taste; and, of course, lemon juice is indispensable to many cocktails.

Dried onion flakes are a boon if you forget to buy fresh onions or if the ones you have bought have secretly sprouted leaves. Add flakes to meat loaves, hamburgers, and meat balls; to soups, instant potato mixes, and gravies; sprinkle over roasts; use where-ever fresh onions are called for. Buy dried onion flakes in the large shaker jar since the tiny sprinkler size only holds several tablespoonfuls.

Dried parsley flakes can be added to soups, gravies, and chopped meat dishes. Use it as a companion to onion flakes in almost every type of dish. It will add subtle flavor and color to your cooking.

A plump head of garlic costs only pennies and will keep for many weeks. Peel a clove or two and dice fine or press through a garlic press and add it to the hot oil when you are browning stew meat, pot roasts, veal, and lamb roasts. Add garlic to hot oil when frying shrimp scampi; use it in a meat ball mixture as a zesty flavoring. Remember not to use too much garlic unless, of course, a healthy amount coincides with your family's taste preferences. Wash your hands with soap and water after handling garlic to avoid an unpleasant odor lingering on your fingertips.

Bay leaves and basil have a great affinity for tomatoes. Add bay leaf to tomato based soups; add it to pot roast in the sur-rounding gravy, but remove the leaf before serving. A pinch of basil will perk up tomato based soups; it can be sprinkled over tomatoes before broiling; and it is also excellent in spaghetti sauces.

Grated lemon peel is available in a small shaker jar. Sprinkle it over poultry and fish as a matter of habit, along with the other seasonings your recipe calls for. It can also be added to cake mixes for an extra lemony flavor, and it will perk up green vegetables when added with a pat of butter.

Paprika is indispensable. Sprinkle it on roasts for flavor and to provide a richer brown crust. Get into the habit of using a dash of paprika for color over bland-looking foods, such as mashed potatoes, herring in cream sauce, or any creamed food that would otherwise blend into the serving platter. Gently now, use a light touch with paprika.

Onion soup mix is the greatest invention for the creative housewife. Of course, used as is and served with floating toasted bread and grated Parmesan cheese, it is a delicious soup. But it has a much greater potential—try it mixed with sour cream for a potato chip dip; sprinkle half a package over a pot roast; add it to homemade soups; or mix it with chopped meat for an unusual meat loaf. Use it a few times and you'll never be without onion soup mix on your shelf.

There are many interesting packaged rice meals on your grocer's shelf. One is a combination white and wild rice which comes with a separate package of seasoned broth. This is a gourmet offering to be served in place of potatoes. It also makes an excellent stuffing for chicken and is especially good smothered with shrimp creole. One package swells up to serve four people, so the price is really not too high.

Muffin mixes are a must for any emergency. Not only are they delicious but they can give you homemade bread in a hurry. Choose the types you prefer and always keep a box or two on the shelf.

A package of dried mashed potatoes is a handy helper, too. Use onion flakes and perhaps a bit of American cheese to kill the processed flavor. Prepare the mashed potatoes as directed on the package, then add a beaten egg and scrape the mixture into a greased casserole. Top with grated American cheese and bake for fifteen minutes in a medium oven. Also, if you add several tablespoons of the dried potato mix to meat loaf you will get the fluffiest meat loaf you ever imagined. Use it to thicken homemade soups and mix it with salmon for salmon croquettes.

Cream of mushroom soup is another indispensable item. As a soup it's delicious; as a sauce it's fabulous! Add a tablespoon of sherry to the undiluted condensed soup and you will have a quick base for chicken à la king. Add American cheese, heat through, and pour over a whole cooked cauliflower. Add a table-spoon of Parmesan cheese to that base and you will have a marvelous sauce for hot baked shrimp or any other bland fish dish. Mix half a can of mushroom soup with a package of cooked

15

chopped spinach and you will have the most delicious creamed spinach. Blend a can of the soup with a package of French-style green beans and a can of French fried onions, bake the mixture for fifteen minutes in a medium oven, and you will produce a green bean dish that brings raves. Cream of celery, cream of chicken, and cream of potato soups are also good choices for the inventive cook looking for tasty time-savers.

Grated Parmesan cheese should be bought in small quantities to insure its freshness. Add it to soups, chopped meat, and fish dishes. It is, of course, a necessity for spaghetti and other pasta dishes. A tablespoon or two can perk up a bland cream sauce, too.

Besides its sweetening power, brown sugar has a flavor all its own. Sprinkle it over carrots or canned sweet potatoes with a dab of butter, and heat through. Bake apples with brown sugar, cinnamon, and a few raisins in the cored-out center. Add brown sugar to cooking cabbage and to canned prepared baked beans.

Canned crab meat is another versatile staple. It can be broken up and mixed into a salad; served on toast with Newburg sauce; or sautéed gently in garlic, onion, and parsley and served as a hot crab meat dish. Not an inexpensive item, but one can will stretch to serve two people. If enough shrimp are added to the dish one can will serve four.

Canned mushrooms, either sliced or whole, are a welcome addition to many vegetables such as peas, green beans, and cauliflower. With sautéed onions, mushrooms do wonders for steak and hamburgers. They lend character to gravies and are an inexpensive item to keep on hand. Of course, fresh mushrooms are even better, but in this case we are planning an emergency shelf of provisions which you can always keep on hand.

Canned French fried onions are an instantly available crumbled topping for vegetable casseroles as well as being an interesting side dish to any beef menu. They are a crunchy flavorful addition to creamed soups used as sauces.

A staple list could be as long as your grocer's aisles. My suggestions are intended to spark your desire to find convenience food products and to use them in new ways of your own invention. Any product that will save you time and make your dinners more interesting will be a happy addition to your staple shelves.

In the current quibbling over whether married women should be called homemakers or housewives, an important aspect of their versatility is being overlooked. A woman who cuts costs and manages her household with a maximum of efficiency and a minimum of effort is certainly a HOME ENGINEER who has earned her MRS. degree Summa Cum Laude.

SUGGESTED EQUIPMENT

Set of mixing bowls
Set of measuring cups
Set of measuring spoons
Set of hanging utensils,
    including:
  Slotted spoon
  Mixing spoon
  Fork
  Pancake turner
  Soup ladle
  Spatula
Set of wooden mixing spoons
Set of knives
Grater
Flour sifter
Bread board
Rolling pin
Colander
Set of strainers
Rubber scraper
Vegetable peeler
Can opener
Kitchen scissors
Bottle opener with corkscrew
Wire whisk
Grapefruit knife
Egg slicer
Mouli food chopper
Pastry cutter
Knife sharpener
Pots and pans:
  2 frying pans, large and
    small
  Double boiler

Dutch oven
Potato baker
3 nesting saucepans with
    covers
1 six-quart pot with cover
2 roasting pans
2 cookie sheets
2 jelly roll pans
1 nine-inch Pyrex pie plate
1 eleven-inch Pyrex pie plate
1 meat-loaf pan
1 muffin pan, regular-sized
    cups
1 muffin pan, small-sized cups
2 quart-sized casseroles with
    covers
1 pint-sized casserole with
    cover
2 layer cake pans
1 ten-inch springform layer
    pan
1 angel food cake pan
Several interesting gelatin
    molds
Electric equipment:
  Toaster
  Blender
  Mixer, with attachments
  Coffee maker
  Warming tray
  Broiler oven
  Deep fryer (optional)
  Electric can opener
    (optional)

17

❧ 5 ❧

Common Knowledge

NEW COOKS OFTEN BECOME FRUSTRATED BY THE OVERWHELMING amount of information that is needed to understand recipes and their directions. What experienced cooks take for granted is something like a new language for the novice. To help you hurdle those first difficult days, read this chapter several times and consider it a foreign vocabulary list. You will see how quickly you learn to think in this new language.

I have never met a good cook who was not also very bright. It takes a clever girl with good executive ability to learn how to take the best advantage of available products without spending forever at the stove. No smart girl would attempt to converse intelligently in a new language unless she had a working knowledge of its rudiments. Since eating is a habit we cannot live without, here is a head start to acquiring what is common knowledge in the world of food.

COOKING METHODS

BAKE	To cook in the oven with dry heat.
BARBECUE	To cook over an open fire, usually outdoors.

BASTE	To moisten baking food with melted fat, gravy, or wine during cooking.
BEAT	To mix ingredients briskly until smooth.
BLANCH	To immerse food quickly in boiling water, then in icy water, in order to remove the skins of fruits, vegetables, or nuts. This technique is also used to stop enzyme action before freezing fresh vegetables and fruit.
BLEND	To combine two or more ingredients with a spoon or with an electric blender, until the ingredients are indistinguishable.
BOIL	To cook in hot bubbling liquid (212 degrees F.). A rapid boil refers to vigorous bubbling, a low boil refers to gentle bubbling.
BRAISE	To brown meat in hot fat, searing all sides, and with a small amount of liquid added to cover and simmer for a long period of time.
BREAD	To dip food in crumbs until complete surface is covered.
BREW	To let stand in hot liquid until flavor is extracted.
BROIL	To expose food to direct heat, by cooking directly under or over a flame or heating element.
CANDY	To glaze fruits or vegetables with a sugar syrup.
CARAMELIZE	To cook sugar over a low heat, stirring until the sugar melts and turns light brown.
CHOP	To cut food into fine pieces.
CREAM	To mix fat and sugar together until the mixture is soft and fluffy, usually done with an electric mixer or with the back of a spoon.
CUBE	To divide into small squares.
CUT	To divide foods with a knife, or to make pastry by cutting fat into flour until small particles result.

DEVIL	To add condiments to food, making it spicy hot.
DICE	To cut food into fine cubes.
DREDGE	To coat food with flour until surface is completely covered.
DUST	To sprinkle food lightly with a dry ingredient, such as flour or sugar.
FILLET	To remove bones from meat or fish.
FLAKE	To break food into flat pieces, usually done with a fork.
FLAMBÉ	To set food ablaze.
FOLD	To mix food from the bottom of the bowl to the top in an under-over motion that distributes the ingredients without destroying the air bubbles.
FRICASSEE	To stew meat in gravy, cooking it a long time over low heat.
FRY	To cook in melted fat.
GLAZE	To cover food with a substance that will create a shiny finish.
GRATE	To rub food against a rough cutting surface, creating tiny particles.
GRILL	To cook by broiling on a rack.
GRIND	To work food into small particles with a food chopper or blender.
JULIENNE	To cut food into slender strips.
KNEAD	To fold, press, and stretch dough until it becomes smooth and elastic.
LARD	To cover lean meat or fish with strips of fat, or to insert fat into the meat with a larding needle.
MARINATE	To soak food in a mixture containing oil, wine, or vinegar, and seasonings for tenderizing and flavoring.

MINCE	To chop food very fine.
MIX	To combine foods together.
MOLD	To shape food by pouring into a desired container and then, when the shape is set, removing from the container.
PANBROIL	To cook meat in an uncovered skillet, pouring off fat as it is rendered.
PANFRY	To cook meat in an uncovered skillet, using a small amount of fat.
PARBOIL	To cook food partway in boiling water.
PARE	To cut off the peels of fruits and vegetables.
PEEL	To strip off the skins of fruits.
POACH	To simmer in hot liquid.
PUREE	To blend or force food through a strainer until it is a smooth sauce.
REDUCE	To boil a liquid down to a smaller quantity.
RENDER	To heat fat until it melts and can be poured free of connective tissue.
ROAST	To cook in an oven.
ROUX	A mixture formed by cooking flour and butter together, and then adding liquid. For a brown sauce, you must brown the roux before adding the liquid.
SAUTÉ	To cook food in a small quantity of fat, usually in a skillet on top of the range, until the desired degree of brownness is attained.
SCALD	To heat liquid to a point just below boiling.
SCORE	To make cuts across the surface of food before roasting.
SEAR	To brown fast, sealing in the juices, either over high heat or in a hot oven.

SIMMER	To cook in liquid, just below the boiling point, using low heat to maintain the temperature.
SKEWER	To pierce food on long pins before cooking.
SKIM	To remove floating fatty substances from liquid, usually done with a spoon.
SLIVER	To cut food into thin pieces.
STEAM	To cook food over, but not touching, boiling water.
STEW	To cook food in liquid over low heat for a long time.
STIR	To mix ingredients with a slow circular motion.
WHIP	To beat rapidly, inflating the volume of the ingredients.

WEIGHTS AND MEASURES

⅓ of ½ teaspoon . . . . Pinch
½ of ¼ teaspoon . . . . ⅛ teaspoon
3 teaspoons . . . . 1 tablespoon
2 tablespoons . . . . ⅛ cup
4 tablespoons . . . . ¼ cup
5 tablespoons, 1 teaspoon . . . . ⅓ cup
8 tablespoons . . . . ½ cup
10 tablespoons, 2 teaspoons . . . . . . ⅔ cup
12 tablespoons . . . . ¾ cup
16 tablespoons . . . . 1 cup
1 cup . . . . 8 fluid ounces
2 cups . . . . 1 pint
2 pints . . . . 1 quart
4 cups . . . . 1 quart
4 quarts . . . . 1 gallon
8 quarts . . . . 1 peck
4 pecks . . . . 1 bushel
16 ounces, dry measure . . . . 1 pound

PROPORTIONAL MEASUREMENTS

Butter or margarine..1 stick or ¼ pound.. ½ cup
Butter or margarine..1 pound ....2 cups
Cheddar cheese .....½ pound ....2 cups grated
Cream cheese ....3 ounces ....6 tablespoons
Egg whites ....8 to 11 whites ......1 cup
Egg yolks ....12 to 14 yolks ......1 cup
All purpose flour ....1 pound ....4 cups sifted
Cake flour ....1 pound ....4¾ cups sifted
Lemon juice ....1 medium lemon ...3 tablespoons juice
Lemon rind ....1 medium lemon ...1 tablespoon grated
                                        rind
Orange juice ....1 medium orange .. ⅓ cup juice
Orange rind ....1 medium orange ..2 tablespoons grated
                                        rind
Walnuts ....1 pound unshelled ..1⅔ cups chopped
                                        nuts
Granulated sugar ....1 pound ....2¼ to 2½ cups
Brown sugar ....1 pound ....2¼ to 2⅓ cups
Confectioners' sugar ..1 pound ....About 4½ cups
Rice ....1 cup raw ....3 to 3½ cups cooked

MEASURING HINTS

LIQUIDS To measure liquids, use a 1-cup measuring cup with space above the 1-cup line, to avoid spilling. Check measurement at eye level. It is convenient to own a 2-cup and a 1-quart measuring cup also.

DRY INGREDIENTS To measure dry ingredients, use a set of 4 graduated measuring cups of ¼ cup, ⅓ cup, ½ cup, and 1 cup. Level off measurements with the edge of a knife.

SPOONFULS To measure spoonfuls, use a set of standard measuring spoons, including ¼ teaspoon, ½ teaspoon, 1 teaspoon, and 1 tablespoon. Level off measurements with the edge of a knife.

CUPS

To measure cups, fill measuring cups lightly; do not pack or shake down (especially flour). Level off with edge of knife. Brown sugar is the exception to the rule; spoon brown sugar into a measuring cup, packing it down with the back of a spoon just enough so it holds its shape when turned out.

SHORTENING

To measure shortening, fill cup first with the difference in water between the amount of shortening desired and 1 cup. For example, if you need ⅔ cup shortening, fill the cup ⅓ full of water and add shortening until the cup is full. Pour off water before adding shortening to recipe.

❧ 6 ❧

Know Your Seasoning Shelf

BEFORE YOU WERE MARRIED, THE WORD SEASON MAY HAVE BROUGHT to mind only a change of apparel and activities—New Year's Eve, skiing and ice-skating, the Spring Prom, tennis and summer sailing, football cheering, and Christmas vacation. Some activities are bland, some tangy, some have lingering memories, and some are better forgotten. So it is with herbs and spices.

Let's face it, you could probably pop a chicken just as is into the oven and serve it to the tune of, "Mmm, this is good," or "Mmm, pass the salt," or "Mmm, this tastes a little flat, dear." We don't want to take chances. That is why we add certain seasonings to certain dishes: to guarantee good taste every time.

While it is important to be adventurous and creative in the kitchen, when it comes to seasoning food you must have a clear understanding of which seasonings will complement a particular dish. And don't get carried away—a little pinch of herbs goes a long way, while too many different varieties in the same pot might "muddy" the flavor. Follow recipes until you acquire the knack of taste-testing and the knowledge of how to improve the flavor of each dish. You will quickly reach this stage if you take the time to understand what you are doing and why you are doing it. You might as well make the attempt for you'll be eating your own cooking for a lifetime. Why not make it interesting?

ALLSPICE — Flavor tastes like a blend of nutmeg, cinnamon, and cloves. It is used with fruit in salads and pies and in some meat and fish dishes.

BASIL, sweet — Flavor is sweetish. Gives additional depth to dishes cooked with tomatoes; used in some soups, some sauces, and some salads.

BAY LEAF — Large dried leaf of considerable flavor for pot roasts, stews, and some meaty soups.

CARAWAY — An herb with aromatic seeds which belongs to the parsley family. Used to flavor breads, cheeses, meat stews, and some vegetables.

CARDAMON — Aromatic seed of plant belonging to the ginger family. Sold ground or whole. Used in Indian and Scandinavian cookery, and in curries and pastries for a sweet pungent flavor.

CAYENNE PEPPER — Also called chili pepper. It is very hot and red in color. Use sparingly in some meat dishes, some sauces, and some cheese dishes.

CHERVIL — Subtle pleasant flavor, used in soups, egg dishes, and in some vegetables.

CHILI POWDER — A blend of spices used to season Mexican dishes, sauces, stews, and some meats.

CHIVES — Slender green tips of an onion-related plant. Used in salads, potato soups, with sour cream as a potato topping, in delicate sauces, and in some cheese dishes.

CINNAMON — Sold ground or in stick form. Used in fruit compotes, fruit pies, some puddings and desserts, and in meats.

CLOVES — Sweet pungent flavor, sold whole or ground. Used in pickling and in ham, tongue, desserts, mulled wines, and teas.

CURRY POWDER	A blend of many spices, herbs, and seeds, with a hot spicy flavor. Used in some sauces, soups, stews, and seafood dishes.
DILL	Used in making dill pickles, in soups, salads, and seafood dishes. Very interesting with potted chicken.
GARLIC	Used fresh in cloved heads, or dried in powder or salt form. Used to season meats, seafood dishes, chicken, and sauces.
GINGER	Sweet and spicy flavor, sold whole or ground. Used to flavor pies, baking goods, and some meat dishes; used frequently in oriental cookery.
MACE	The outer shell of the nutmeg with a flavor similar to nutmeg. Used in baking, some meat and fish dishes, sauces, pumpkin dishes, and in some vegetables in small amounts.
MARJORAM	Sold whole or ground. Used in vegetables, soups, lamb dishes, and some stuffings.
MINT	Used in jellies, sauces, candies, some desserts, and some meat dishes.
MUSTARD	Hot sharp flavor, sold in seed, powdered, or prepared form. Used in cheese, meat, and fish dishes, and as a condiment.
NUTMEG	Sold whole or ground. Used in baking, puddings, sauces, vegetables, fruit. and meat dishes.
OREGANO	A wild sweet marjoram with a strong and pleasantly bitter taste. Used in many Mexican, Italian, and Spanish dishes. Used with tomatoes, in soups, salads, sauces, and meat dishes.
PAPRIKA	Red powder with slightly sweet taste. Used as a garnish, on roasts, in seafood dishes, and in soups.
PARSLEY	Mild distinctively flavored green leaves. Used with fish, meat, soups, sauces, and as a garnish.

HERBS AND SPICES AND WHERE TO USE THEM

PEPPER, black	Buy whole and grind fresh for each use in meat, fish, and soups.
PEPPER, white	Less pungent than black pepper. Used in white sauces and may be used interchangeably with black pepper.
ROSEMARY	Fresh sweet-flavored leaves. Used in lamb dishes, vegetables, sauces, and soups.
SAFFRON	Fragrant and slightly bitter yellow-orange filaments. Used for color in rice, sauces, and some soups.
SAGE	Strongly aromatic dried leaf, sold whole or ground. Used in stuffings, in some soups, some sauces, and some meat dishes.
SAVORY, summer	Used in vegetables, salads, sauces, and egg cookery.
TARRAGON	A slightly licorice flavor, used to enhance sauces, chicken, eggs, and meat dishes.
THYME	Warm aromatic flavor. Used in chowders, stuffings, salads, tomatoes, cheeses, and with some fruits.
TURMERIC	Related to the ginger family but has its own distinctive flavor. Used in curries, fish dishes, sauces, and pickle mixtures.

VEGETABLES AND THEIR COMPLEMENTING SPICES

ASPARAGUS
Basil	Savory
Marjoram	Tarragon
Nutmeg	Thyme

BEANS
Basil	Nutmeg
Chives	Oregano
Curry powder	Savory
Dill	Thyme
Mint	

BEETS
Allspice	Marjoram
Basil	Mint
Bay leaf	Nutmeg
Cloves	Tarragon
Dill	Thyme

BROCCOLI
Basil	Nutmeg
Curry powder	Oregano

VEGETABLES AND THEIR COMPLEMENTING SPICES

BRUSSELS SPROUTS
Basil	Nutmeg
Curry powder	Sage
Dill	Savory
Marjoram	

CABBAGE
Allspice	Curry powder
Basil	Dill
Bay leaf	Nutmeg
Cloves	Tarragon

CARROTS
Allspice	Ginger
Basil	Mace
Bay leaf	Marjoram
Chervil	Mint
Chili powder	Nutmeg
Cloves	Rosemary
Dill	Thyme

CAULIFLOWER
Basil	Nutmeg
Chives	Paprika
Mace	Rosemary

CELERY
Basil	Marjoram

CORN
Cayenne	Paprika
Curry powder	

EGGPLANT
Allspice	Rosemary
Chili powder	Sage
Dill	Savory
Oregano	Thyme

MUSHROOMS
Chives	Tarragon
Oregano	Thyme
Rosemary	

ONIONS
Basil	Oregano
Chili powder	Paprika
Curry powder	Rosemary
Ginger	Sage
Marjoram	Thyme
Nutmeg	

PEAS
Basil	Mint
Chervil	Mustard, dry
Chives	Nutmeg
Ginger	Oregano
Marjoram	Rosemary

POTATOES
Basil	Mace
Bay leaf	Mint
Caraway seed	Paprika
Chili powder	Parsley
Chives	Rosemary
Curry powder	Sage
Dill	Thyme

SPINACH
Allspice	Mint
Basil	Nutmeg
Dill	Oregano
Mace	Rosemary
Marjoram	Thyme

VEGETABLES AND THEIR COMPLEMENTING SPICES

SUMMER SQUASH

Basil	Nutmeg
Curry	Rosemary
Marjoram	Sage

SWEET POTATOES

Cinnamon	Mace
Ginger	Nutmeg

TOMATOES

Allspice	Marjoram
Basil	Oregano
Bay leaf	Sage
Chives	Tarragon
Dill	Thyme

WHITE TURNIPS

Basil	Dill
Caraway seed	Rosemary
Chili powder	Thyme

YELLOW SQUASH

Allspice	Cloves
Cinnamon	Nutmeg

YELLOW TURNIPS

Basil	Savory
Rosemary	Thyme

ZUCCHINI

Basil	Oregano
Marjoram	Thyme

FRUITS AND THEIR COMPLEMENTING SPICES

APPLES

Cinnamon	Mace
Cloves	Nutmeg
Ginger	

APRICOTS

Cinnamon	Cloves

BANANAS

Nutmeg

BLUEBERRIES

Cinnamon	Nutmeg
Cloves	

CHERRIES

Allspice	Ginger
Cinnamon	Nutmeg
Cloves	

CRANBERRIES

Allspice	Ginger
Cinnamon	Nutmeg
Cloves	

FIGS

Allspice	Ginger
Cinnamon	

GRAPEFRUIT

Cardamon	Ginger
Cinnamon	Nutmeg

LEMON

Cloves	Nutmeg
Mace	

LIME
Cloves   Nutmeg
Mace

MELON
Cardamon   Mint

ORANGES
Cardamon   Mint

PEACHES
Allspice   Ginger
Cinnamon   Mace
Cloves

PEARS
Cinnamon   Ginger
Cloves

PINEAPPLE
Cinnamon   Mint
Ginger   Nutmeg
Mace

PLUMS
Cinnamon   Cloves

PRUNES
Cinnamon   Cloves

RHUBARB
Allspice   Ginger
Cinnamon   Nutmeg
Cloves

7

Breakfast Inspirations

KICK THE DAY OFF TO A GOOD START! TRAIN YOURSELF TO REACH for your comb and lipstick, a bottle of cologne, and a fetching little something to wear. If you remember to pay a visit to the kitchen a few minutes before bedtime, you will enter it the next morning with your job half done. At night, set the table, prepare the juice, and decide what the morning menu will be. There is nothing nicer than to plan a bit of leisure into your early morning chores.

Some planning the night before will prevent the blind groping with half-closed eyes for the same old box of dry cereal you have been serving every day. If it has to be those crunchies, at least add slices of banana or peach and serve with a small pitcher of milk. Vary the juice that precedes it, and alternate the jelly for toast. Vary the bread to be toasted. One morning it might be raisin toast, sprinkled with a feather dusting of cinnamon. Or perhaps the special muffins you've stored in the freezer.

Eggs, too, do not have to be served the same old way every day. With the vast array of foodstuffs at her fingertips, the American housewife can afford to be imaginative at every meal. Scoop out an English muffin and bake an egg in it. Put a slice of American cheese over scrambled eggs and let it melt a moment. Fry an egg sunny-side-up on top of a slice of ham. Breakfasts won't ever be monotonous unless you don't care enough.

The picture your husband carries with him throughout the day is not necessarily the one in his wallet or on his desk. It is the memory of the last time he saw you. Will it be a hasty goodbye to a grunting lump of blankets? Or a frowsy touseled-haired ghost who haunts the kitchen every morning with the same dull fare? If he is lucky, perhaps he will remember a wife with a smiling scrubbed face cheerfully waving goodbye at the door. He's off to slay a few dragons, confident that his home is in good order for the day. If he's very lucky, he might find a surprise note tucked away in a pocket to remind him how much you care.

An old saying tells us that a man represents a sturdy oak, and a woman a clinging vine. She wraps herself around him, leaning on his strength, but when lightning strikes, she tightly binds his wounds and holds him together. Your wifely job does not begin when you open your eyes in the morning—it begins when your husband opens his!

Idealistic? Perhaps. But with fifteen-thousand-plus breakfasts ahead of you before that golden wedding day, one third of the meals you eat does become an important item on the balance sheet of marriage.

The recipes in this chapter are quick to prepare and have been chosen for their novelty as well as their nutritional value. They deserve your consideration, for breakfast is truly the start of things.

HOW TO BUY AND STORE EGGS

The color of eggs does not affect their quality or taste. Buy the eggs that are freshest and cheapest.

Fresh eggs can be determined by their rough chalky exterior; old eggs are smooth and shiny. A fresh egg will sink in water. If you hold the egg up to the light, the yolk should be in the center. When you break an egg as for frying, the yolk should sit high above and in the center of a thick ring of white, which in itself stands high above the rest of the white. The farther toward the edges the higher white slips, the older the egg.

To store eggs do not wash them; water destroys the protective film which repels air and odors. Store promptly in the refrigerator, since eggs lose their flavor quickly at room temperature. Store in the original carton or in a covered container. Eggs left uncovered lose moisture through their porous shell.

To store extra whites or yolks cover yolks with cold water and store in refrigerator for several days; place leftover whites in a jar, cover tightly, and store in refrigerator for several days.

Egg sizes are determined by the weight of eggs, not by their quality. There are about three ounces' difference between each size of eggs: Small eggs weigh at least eighteen ounces per dozen, medium eggs weigh at least twenty-one ounces per dozen, large eggs weigh at least twenty-four ounces per dozen, and extra-large eggs weigh at least twenty-seven ounces per dozen. Smaller eggs sell for less than larger eggs because you are buying them by weight. Sometimes it is better value to buy a smaller-sized egg. Check the price and the weight to determine whether one size is being offered at a better price.

HOW TO COOK EGGS

To boil eggs choose a saucepan that is deep enough for water to cover eggs completely.

To soft-cook eggs bring the water to a boil, reduce heat to just below simmering, and place eggs in the water with a slotted spoon. Cook for 2 to 4 minutes, depending on desired doneness.

To hard-cook eggs bring the water to a boil, reduce heat to just below simmering, and place eggs in the water with a slotted spoon. Cook for 12 to 15 minutes, depending on desired doneness.

To poach eggs fill a skillet with water, bringing it to a rolling boil. Reduce heat to simmering, add a teaspoon of vinegar, and break each egg carefully into the water. If white spreads, push it toward the center with a spoon. Cook for 4 minutes or less depending on desired doneness. Remove egg with a slotted spoon. Serve on toast or English muffin half.

To fry eggs heat butter in a skillet, break each egg carefully into the skillet, and cook on low heat to desired doneness. If you prefer fried eggs with a thin film over the yolk, spoon a bit of white over the yolk and cover the pan during the last few minutes of cooking. Remove with a spatula.

To scramble eggs heat butter in a skillet and pour in an egg mixture consisting of 1 tablespoon of milk to each beaten egg. Reduce heat to low. When mixture sets around the edges, push gently toward the center, allowing uncooked mixture to flow toward the edges and set. Cook until mixture is set but still moist.

ZESTY SCRAMBLED EGGS

To serve 2 or 3	*To serve 4 to 6*
1 *tablespoon butter*	2 *tablespoons butter*
4 *eggs*	8 *eggs*
¼ *cup milk*	½ *cup milk*
¼ *teaspoon salt*	½ *teaspoon salt*
⅛ *teaspoon pepper*	¼ *teaspoon pepper*
2 *slices American cheese, diced*	4 *slices American cheese, diced*
2 *tablespoons chopped chives*	4 *tablespoons chopped chives*

Melt butter in a large skillet. Beat eggs. Add milk, salt, pepper, diced American cheese, and most of the chopped chives, reserving about a teaspoonful for garnishing. Pour egg mixture into skillet and cook over medium heat, pushing solidified egg aside and allowing liquid egg to contact the skillet. Cook until eggs are set but still moist, and cheese is partially melted. Garnish with the reserved chopped chives. Serve at once.

CREAMY SCRAMBLED EGGS

To serve 2 or 3	*To serve 4 to 6*
1 *tablespoon butter*	2 *tablespoons butter*
4 *eggs*	8 *eggs*
¼ *teaspoon salt*	½ *teaspoon salt*
⅛ *teaspoon pepper*	¼ *teaspoon pepper*
⅛ *teaspoon thyme*	¼ *teaspoon thyme*
½ *cup dairy sour cream*	1 *cup dairy sour cream*

Melt butter in a large skillet. Beat eggs, salt, pepper, and thyme together until well blended. Pour into skillet. Stir in sour cream. Cook over very low heat, stirring occasionally, until eggs reach desired firmness. Serve at once.

EGGS BENEDICT

For each serving
1 *egg*
½ *English muffin*
1 *thin slice ham*
3 *tablespoons Hollandaise Sauce (see pages 134–35)*
Paprika (optional)

Poach egg according to directions on page 34. Lightly toast English muffin half. Top with ham slice, tucking square corners under to conform to round muffin. Top ham with poached egg. Cover all with Hollandaise Sauce. Sprinkle paprika over top if desired. Serve at once.

BAKED EGG IN A MUFFIN

For each serving
½ *English muffin*
1 *egg*
Dash of salt
Dash of pepper

Scoop out soft center of the English muffin half. Place on a baking pan. Break egg carefully into the muffin cup. Sprinkle with salt and pepper. Bake in a 350-degree oven for about 15 minutes, or until egg reaches desired firmness. Serve at once.

CHEESE OMELET

To serve 2 or 3	*To serve 4 to 6*
3 *eggs*	6 *eggs*
¼ *teaspoon salt*	½ *teaspoon salt*
Dash of pepper	⅛ *teaspoon pepper*
1 *tablespoon butter*	2 *tablespoons butter*
¼ *cup diced American cheese*	⅓ *cup diced American cheese*

Beat eggs slightly; add salt and pepper. Heat butter in an omelet skillet and pour egg mixture into skillet. As egg solidifies, prick the bottom with a fork so liquid egg will flow down and solidify. When omelet is partially done, sprinkle with diced cheese and flip one half of omelet over the other half. Continue cooking for a few minutes. Remove from skillet and serve immediately.

FRENCH TOAST

To serve 2 or 3	To serve 4 to 6
1 egg	2 eggs
⅔ cup milk	1⅓ cups milk
⅛ teaspoon salt	¼ teaspoon salt
4 slices bread	8 slices bread
1 tablespoon butter	2 tablespoons butter
2 teaspoons confectioners' sugar	4 teaspoons confectioners' sugar
Jam (optional)	Jam (optional)
Maple syrup (optional)	Maple syrup (optional)

Beat egg. Add milk and salt. Dip bread into batter and fry in melted butter in a large skillet. Turn over once bottom surface of bread is browned; brown the other side. Serve immediately with a sprinkling of confectioners' sugar or spread with jam or maple syrup.

APPLESAUCE PANCAKES

To serve 2 or 3	To serve 4 to 6
¾ cup sifted flour	1½ cups sifted flour
1 teaspoon baking powder	2 teaspoons baking powder
1 tablespoon sugar	2 tablespoons sugar
¼ teaspoon salt	½ teaspoon salt
1 egg, beaten	1 egg, beaten
⅔ cup milk	1⅔ cups milk
2 tablespoons butter-flavored oil	¼ cup butter-flavored oil
1½ cups applesauce	3 cups applesauce
Powdered sugar	Powdered sugar

Sift together flour, baking powder, sugar, and salt. Combine egg, milk, and butter-flavored oil. Add to dry ingredients, stirring until almost smooth. For each pancake, pour about ¼ cup batter onto hot, ungreased griddle. Cook until the underside is golden brown and bubbles appear on upper surface; turn and cook on other side until golden brown. Place about ¼ cup applesauce in center of each pancake. Roll up and sprinkle with powdered sugar.

BROWN BREAD WITH BACON–CHEESE

To serve 2 or 3
½ *(1-pound) can brown bread*
Butter
4 *slices bacon, cut in half*
4 *slices cheddar cheese*

To serve 4 to 6
1 *(1-pound) can brown bread*
Butter
8 *slices bacon, cut in half*
8 *slices cheddar cheese*

Cut brown bread into ½-inch slices. Toast. Butter one side and put in a broiling pan. Cook bacon until crisp and lay 2 strips on each slice of brown bread. Top with a slice of cheese and put under the broiler until cheese is melted. Serve at once.

❧ 8 ❧

Soup Is Easy

OLD-FASHIONED COOKS WHO USED WOODBURNING BLACK STOVES often kept a huge kettle constantly simmering at the rear of the stove. All the bones, scraps of meat and vegetables, and any leftover cereals were spooned into the pot at the end of each meal, creating an ever-changing hearty soup. Nowadays, with the excellent canned, frozen, and dehydrated soups available, we tend to prepare soups according to the directions on their labels, thankful that such delicious time-saving products have been developed. However, these new products have also stimulated a new culinary technique—the art of using prepared soups so ingeniously that no one suspects their use in a dish. Prepared soups are mixed together and are used as sauces to give vegetables new tastes and appearances, and to change roasts and stews into gourmet dishes.

How you serve a soup is almost as important as the soup itself. Creamed soups, for example, are generally served in smaller portions and may be offered in conversation-piece tiny bowls. Using a tureen and a handsome ladle at the table is a charming touch that adds to the importance of the soup course. Always keep soup garnishes on hand; croutons, popcorn, sour cream, chives, parsley, paprika, Parmesan cheese, thin lemon slices, and even whipped cream can complement the simplest soups. Don't for-

39

get that there are delicious cold soups which may enhance the rest of your menu. Borscht with sour cream or floating diced cucumbers, blender gazpacho, vichyssoise with chives, and canned consomme Madrilène are a few of the many tempting cold soup courses.

Make it a practice to save vegetable juices from cooking water or from canned vegetables. They contain valuable vitamins and may be kept in the refrigerator for several days in a sterilized, tightly covered jar. Use this nourishing liquid in place of water when using condensed soups or as an addition to homemade soups.

How would you start to construct a good pot of soup from scratch? There's nothing magical about homemade soup. Either follow recipes down to the last shake of pepper or rely on your common sense. First the common sense technique: Start with a large pot. Place in it a pound or two of nice meaty beef neck bones, which are inexpensive and will provide both taste and meat. Or start with a turkey carcass, broken into pieces to fit the pot, or a collection of chicken necks, gizzards, and backs. Be sure to begin with some item that will provide a base for a rich soup. Next cover the base with enough water for the amount of ingredients you intend to include. Add several onions, peeled and gashed across the top. Round up a few scraped carrots, some parsley, and a rooty vegetable like a turnip or a parsnip. Some celery stalks with their leaves wouldn't hurt a bit either. If you want to make a beef soup, add a can of tomatoes; if it is to be a poultry soup add a few sprigs of fresh dill. Be discriminating about the things you put in, but don't be overly cautious.

Now what is going to distinguish this potpourri? You have to add a reasonable amount of salt and pepper to bring out some flavor, and perhaps a bit of sugar, too. Add the juice of a lemon if you have used tomatoes. If you want to turn this mixture into a pea soup, now is the time to add a package of dried peas or various dried beans which you have presoaked for several hours. If it's going to be a vegetable soup, now is the time to put the cover on the pot and let it simmer slowly for hours until the liquid has reduced in volume and the soup begins to taste like something. How do you know how it tastes? Taste it! Does it need some more salt or pepper? Add it. Does it still taste flat? Add some bouillon cubes to perk it up. If you are making a vegetable soup, add the vegetables, frozen or fresh, now—vegetables like green beans, chunks of potatoes, or any other that does not have a strong flavor of its own. Cover and simmer some more—until the vegetables are tender. For additional body, add barley, rice, or cooked macaroni. With this kind of soup, almost anything goes!

Without the additions you would have a reduced soup stock, which could be refrigerated and used at a later time. In order to rid homemade soup stock of fat, refrigerate the soup until the fat rises to the top and solidifies into a block. The fat should not be removed, however, until the soup is ready to be used since it forms a seal against bacteria, assuring that the soup stock will remain fresh for several days.

Included in this chapter are basic start-from-scratch soups, combination quick-trick soups, and suggestions for using prepared soups in novel ways. The recipes will allow you to proceed with confidence and ignite your enthusiasm to try some tricks of your own devising. You will find that a soup course lends warmth and dignity to a meal, especially if it is served from an impressive-looking tureen.

CHICKEN SOUP

To serve 6 to 8

1 *soup chicken (fowl), quartered (about 4 pounds)*
2 *quarts water*
1 *whole onion, peeled*
2 *whole carrots, scraped*
4 *stalks celery, including tops*
1 *parsnip root, cleaned*
2 *sprigs parsley*
2 *sprigs dill*
2 *teaspoons salt*
¼ *teaspoon pepper*
2 *teaspoons sugar*

Clean chicken; place it in a deep pot, add water and remaining ingredients, except sugar. Bring to a boil, then simmer covered until chicken is tender, about 2 hours. Remove chicken, strain soup, and chill. Skim off fat which has risen to the top of chilled soup. Reheat soup. Increase seasoning if desired and add sugar. Serve with a piece of soup carrot in each bowl, and with noodles or any other soup accompaniment.

ONION SOUP

To serve 4 to 6
3 *large onions, sliced thin*
3 *tablespoons butter*
2 *(10½-ounce) cans beef consomme*
¼ *teaspoon salt*
⅛ *teaspoon pepper*
Grated Parmesan cheese (optional)

Sauté sliced onions in butter in the bottom of a saucepan until onions are golden. Add beef consomme, salt, and pepper. Simmer for 15 minutes, covered, and serve hot. Pass a small dish of grated Parmesan cheese to be sprinkled on the onion soup if desired.

TOMATO–RICE SOUP

To serve 6 to 8
1 *pound meaty beef neck bones*
2 *quarts water*
2 *cans (approximately 2 pounds each) tomatoes*
2 *onions, diced*
2 *tablespoons brown sugar*
1 *teaspoon salt*
¼ *cup lemon juice*
¼ *teaspoon pepper*
½ *teaspoon basil*
½ *cup instant rice*

Place bones, water, tomatoes, and onions in a large deep pot. Add brown sugar, salt, lemon juice, pepper, and basil. Simmer for 2 hours, covered. Add rice 15 minutes before serving, bringing soup to a boil as directed on the rice package. Then cover and remove from heat. Stir and serve hot.

CABBAGE SOUP

To serve 6 to 8
1 *pound meaty beef neck bones*
2 *quarts water*
1 *teaspoon salt*
2 *onions, sliced*
1 *large can (approximately 2 pounds) tomatoes*
1 *can tomato paste*
1 *medium head cabbage, sliced thin*
¼ *cup lemon juice*
2 *tablespoons brown sugar*
½ *teaspoon pepper*
8 *gingersnap cookies*

Place bones, water, and salt in a large deep pot and bring to a boil. Skim surface with a large spoon to remove residue. Turn heat low and add onions, tomatoes, tomato paste, cabbage, lemon juice, brown sugar, and pepper. Simmer for 2 hours. Taste, and add additional lemon juice or sugar as needed to obtain the balanced sweet and sour taste desired. Crumble gingersnaps into the soup and simmer for an additional 15 minutes.

FISH CHOWDER

To serve 6 to 8
2 *cups water*
2 *pounds fish fillets*
4 *onions, sliced*
4 *potatoes, peeled and diced*
4 *cups milk*
1 *cup heavy cream*
¼ *cup butter*
1 *teaspoon salt*
½ *teaspoon black pepper*

Boil water in a deep saucepan; add fish fillets and simmer covered for about 10 minutes. Remove fish. Add onions and potatoes to fish-water in saucepan; cover and simmer for 10 minutes. Add milk, cream, butter, salt, and pepper. Flake cooked fish and return to the saucepan. Heat over very low heat, stirring occasionally. Serve hot.

MANHATTAN CLAM CHOWDER

To serve 2 or 3	*To serve 4 to 6*
2 *slices bacon*	2 *slices bacon*
1 *small onion, diced*	1 *large onion, diced*
1 *stalk celery, diced*	2 *stalks celery, diced*
½ *green pepper, diced*	1 *green pepper, diced*
1 *carrot, diced*	2 *carrots, diced*
1 *medium potato, cubed*	2 *medium potatoes, cubed*
½ *teaspoon salt*	1 *teaspoon salt*
¼ *teaspoon pepper*	½ *teaspoon pepper*
1 *cup water*	2 *cups water*
1½ *cups canned tomatoes, with juice*	3 *cups canned tomatoes, with juice*
¼ *teaspoon thyme*	½ *teaspoon thyme*
1 *can minced clams*	2 *cans minced clams*

Fry bacon in the bottom of a deep saucepan. Remove bacon strips and use for another purpose. To the bacon fat add the diced onion and sauté until golden. Add diced celery, diced green pepper, diced carrots, cubed potatoes, salt, pepper, water, tomatoes, and thyme. Stir, cover, and simmer for 30 to 40 minutes, or until all vegetables are tender. Add clams, heat through, and serve hot.

SPLIT PEA SOUP

A QUICK-TRICK WAY

To serve 6 to 8
1 *pound meaty beef neck bones*
2 *quarts water*
1 *(7-ounce) package split peas*
1 *package dehydrated onion soup mix*
Pepper (optional)

Place washed bones in a large pot. Add water, split peas, and the contents of the onion soup mix. The onion soup mix is already seasoned, so it is not necessary to add anything except pepper if you wish. Stir. Simmer for 2 hours, covered, stirring occasionally. Remove bones; remove meat from the bones and cut into small chunks; return the chunks of meat to the soup if you wish to serve a hearty soup.

GAZPACHO

A QUICK-TRICK WAY

To serve 4

1 (10½-ounce) can condensed cream of tomato soup

2 tablespoons wine vinegar

1 clove garlic, minced

1 cup water

2 tablespoons olive oil

1 cucumber, cut up

½ onion, cut up

½ green pepper, cut up

1 teaspoon sugar

½ teaspoon salt

¼ teaspoon pepper

Place all ingredients in an electric blender. Blend well. Chill. Serve cold.

ONION–SALMON SOUP

A QUICK-TRICK WAY

To serve 2 or 3	To serve 4 to 6
3 tablespoons butter	⅓ cup butter
2 large onions, sliced thin	4 large onions, sliced thin
1 (3¼-ounce) can salmon	1 (7¾-ounce) can salmon
⅛ teaspoon pepper	¼ teaspoon pepper
1 (10½-ounce) can beef consomme	2 (10½-ounce) cans beef consomme
French bread	French bread
1 tablespoon grated Parmesan cheese	2 tablespoons grated Parmesan cheese

45

In a large saucepan, melt butter and sauté onions until they are transparent. Drain salmon, reserving liquid. Flake salmon and add to onions. Add salmon liquid, pepper, and beef consomme; bring to a boil and simmer for 10 minutes. Pour into individual oven-proof soup casseroles. Top each with a slice of French bread and sprinkle with Parmesan cheese. Broil 3 to 4 inches from heat for several minutes until cheese is lightly browned. Serve at once.

VICHYSSOISE

A QUICK-TRICK WAY

To serve 2 or 3	*To serve 4 to 6*
1 *chicken bouillon cube*	2 *chicken bouillon cubes*
¼ *cup boiling water*	½ *cup boiling water*
1 *(10¼-ounce) can frozen cream of potato soup*	2 *(10¼-ounce) cans frozen cream of potato soup*
1 *cup milk*	2 *cups milk*
2 *tablespoons chopped chives*	¼ *cup chopped chives*
½ *cup dairy sour cream*	1 *cup dairy sour cream*

Dissolve bouillon cubes in boiling water. Combine with potato soup, milk, and chives in a saucepan; stir constantly over low heat until soup is thawed. Remove from heat and beat with a rotary beater or in a blender until smooth. Beat in sour cream. Refrigerate until well chilled, about 4 hours. Serve cold, with a sprinkling of chopped chives.

CLAM BISQUE

A QUICK-TRICK WAY

To serve 4 to 6

1 *(10½-ounce) can condensed cream of celery soup*
1 *(10½-ounce) can white clam sauce*
¼ *teaspoon thyme*
1 *cup water*
Parsley (optional)
Paprika (optional)

Empty cream of celery soup into a saucepan. Add white clam sauce, thyme, and water. Stir well. Heat for 5 minutes and serve

46

hot. Garnish with a sprig of parsley or a dash of paprika, if desired.

LOBSTER BISQUE

A QUICK-TRICK WAY

To serve 6 to 8

1 (10½-ounce) can condensed cream of mushroom soup

1 (10½-ounce) can condensed cream of asparagus soup

1 soup can light cream

1 can (about 4 ounces) lobster meat, cut up

2 tablespoons sherry

In a saucepan, combine cream of mushroom soup and cream of asparagus soup. Stir in light cream. Add lobster meat. Add sherry. Heat thoroughly without boiling. Serve at once.

CREAMED CELERY–NOODLE SOUP

A QUICK-TRICK WAY

To serve 4 to 6

1 (10½-ounce) can condensed cream of celery soup

1 (10½-ounce) can condensed chicken noodle soup

1½ cups water

½ cup milk

⅛ teaspoon dried dillweed

In a saucepan, combine cream of celery soup and chicken noodle soup. Add water and milk, stirring until smooth. Add dillweed. Simmer for 5 minutes, stirring occasionally. Serve hot.

CREAMED PUREE OF MONGOL SOUP

A QUICK-TRICK WAY

To serve 4 to 6

1 (10½-ounce) can condensed cream of tomato soup

1 (10½-ounce) can condensed green pea soup

1 soup can of water

1 soup can of milk

½ teaspoon dried basil

Sour cream (optional)

In a saucepan, combine tomato soup and pea soup. Add water and milk, stirring until smooth. Add basil. Simmer for 5 minutes, stirring occasionally. Serve hot, with a dollop of sour cream if desired.

9

Delicious Fish

FISH CAN BE A FASCINATING SOURCE OF VITAMINS, MINERALS, PRO-
tein, and low-calorie dining. It can be deep-fried, sautéed,
poached, broiled, or baked. Edible fish are divided into three
categories: saltwater fish, freshwater fish, and shellfish. All can
be prepared to tempt even the fussiest of palates.

You can tell whether or not fish is fresh by pushing your finger
into the skin of a whole one. There should be no mark of indenta-
tion left from your finger pressure. Look at the eyes: they should
be bright, clear, and bulging. The gills should be bright red. The
odor should be sea fresh; an off smell should not be tolerated.
Fresh fish should be cooked as soon as possible, making the trip
from the sea to the table in the shortest time possible. Be careful not to overcook fish, for it will become dry and unpalatable.
Frozen fish is usually sold in fillets, and should be kept in a frozen
state until just before using.

When buying a whole fish allot one pound per person, allowing for waste due to the trimming of head, entrails, and bones.
For dressed fish (already trimmed) allow from one-third to
one-half pound per person.

Fresh shrimp may be shelled and deveined either before or
after boiling, but they will hold their shape better if cleaned
beforehand. Excellent frozen shrimp which has been precleaned

and flash frozen is also available. It can be a real time saver for dishes such as Shrimp Creole. Prebreaded, cleaned frozen shrimp are a good buy and a time saver, too. They are excellent to fry and serve as appetizers or as a main course. Some are split into butterfly shapes with the tails left on to permit deft handling.

Whole lobster should be cooked alive in order to be completely fresh tasting. To avoid the mess and waste of whole lobster, you may prefer to purchase rock lobster tails, either fresh or frozen. They may be poached or broiled, but do not overcook them as the meat will toughen and become tasteless.

Fish should never be boiled actively, but rather poached gently in salted water to which a flavored vinegar such as tarragon or wine vinegar has been added. This will guarantee a more tender, sweeter fish which will hold its shape when removed from the water. The ratio of ingredients is one teaspoon of salt and two tablespoons of vinegar to every quart of water.

Broiled and sautéed fish need quick cooking and immediate serving. They take kindly to butter and lemon juice. Try a generous sprinkling of chopped parsley for an exquisite taste.

Grocery shelves have a generous variety of canned fish—tuna, salmon, cod, sardines, and tomato herring. The refrigerator shelves display jars of herring in wine sauce, herring in sour cream sauce, and pickled salmon and onions. They will help you to diversify your lunch and appetizer offerings. Once opened, refrigerate all canned fish products and use within a day or two.

The recipes in this chapter will give you a head start on collecting other good fish recipes. They are all dependable and geared to the novice fish palate, with just enough bait to hook you on fish for life!

FISH PREPARATION GUIDE

BASS	Bake, broil, fry
BLUEFISH	Bake, broil, fry
BUTTERFISH	Bake, broil, fry
CARP	Bake, broil, fry
CATFISH	Bake, fry
CLAMS	Fry, steam
COD	Bake, broil, poach, fry
CRABS, HARD SHELL	Boil
CRABS, SOFT SHELL	Fry, broil
EEL	Broil, poach, fry

FLOUNDER	Bake, broil, fry
GROUPER	Bake, broil, poach, fry
HADDOCK	Bake, broil, poach, fry
HAKE	Broil, poach
HALIBUT	Bake, broil, poach, fry
HERRING	Bake, broil, poach, fry
LOBSTER	Bake, broil, boil
MACKEREL	Bake, broil, poach, fry
MULLET	Bake, broil, fry
OYSTERS	Bake, broil, fry
PERCH	Bake, broil, fry
PICKEREL	Bake, broil, poach, fry
PIKE	Bake, broil, fry
POMPANO	Bake, broil
RED SNAPPER	Bake, broil, poach, fry
SALMON	Bake, broil, poach, fry
SCALLOPS	Broil, fry
SHAD	Bake, broil, poach, fry
SHRIMP	Boil, broil, fry
SMELT	Bake, broil, fry
STURGEON	Bake, broil, poach
SWORDFISH	Bake, broil, fry
TROUT	Bake, broil, poach, fry
TUNA	Bake, broil, poach
WHITEFISH	Bake, broil, poach, fry
WHITING	Bake, broil, poach, fry

FLOUNDER–BANANA AMANDINE

To serve 2 or 3	*To serve 4 to 6*
1 *pound fillets of flounder*	2 *pounds fillets of flounder*
¼ *teaspoon salt*	½ *teaspoon salt*
Dash of pepper	⅛ *teaspoon pepper*
Bananas, sliced lengthwise	*Bananas, sliced lengthwise*
1 *tablespoon lemon juice*	2 *tablespoons lemon juice*
Almond Butter Sauce	*Almond Butter Sauce*
(see pages 133–34)	*(see pages 133–34)*

Arrange fish fillets in a broiling pan. Season with salt and pepper.
Use half a banana for each slice of fish, arranging them round

side up alongside the fish in the broiler pan. Sprinkle banana with lemon juice. Broil for 6 to 8 minutes, or until fish flakes easily. Remove to a platter, placing broiled banana (round side up) down the center of each slice of fish. Pour Almond Butter Sauce over all. Serve at once.

POACHED SALMON WITH CUCUMBER SAUCE

To serve 2 or 3	*To serve 4 to 6*

3 *slices salmon steak,*
    1 inch thick
	6 *slices salmon steak,*
	    1 inch thick

Boiling water	*Boiling water*
2 *teaspoons tarragon vinegar*	1 *tablespoon tarragon vinegar*
½ *teaspoon salt*	1 *teaspoon salt*
4 *whole black peppercorns*	6 *whole black peppercorns*

Arrange salmon slices in a large skillet. Pour enough boiling water to cover fish. Add vinegar, salt, and whole black peppercorns. Simmer for about 10 minutes, or until salmon is tender but still holds its shape. Remove carefully to a platter and serve with cucumber sauce.

SAUCE:	SAUCE:
1 *teaspoon chopped parsley*	2 *teaspoons chopped parsley*
1 *teaspoon chopped chives*	2 *teaspoons chopped chives*
¼ *cucumber, chopped*	½ *cucumber, chopped*
¼ *cup mayonnaise*	½ *cup mayonnaise*

Stir chopped parsley, chopped chives, and chopped cucumber into mayonnaise.

BROILED SOLE SMITANE

To serve 2 or 3	*To serve 4 to 6*
1 *pound fillets of sole*	2 *pounds fillets of sole*
1 *tablespoon lemon juice*	2 *tablespoons lemon juice*
¼ *cup dairy sour cream*	½ *cup dairy sour cream*
1 *tablespoon chopped chives*	2 *tablespoons chopped chives*
¼ *teaspoon paprika*	½ *teaspoon paprika*

Arrange fish fillets in a broiling pan. Sprinkle with lemon juice. Spread a coating of sour cream on fish. Top with a sprinkling of chopped chives and paprika. Broil for 6 to 8 minutes, or until fish flakes easily. Serve at once.

FISH CREOLE

A QUICK-TRICK WAY

To serve 2 or 3
2 *tablespoons butter*
1 *onion, diced*
1 *green pepper, diced*
1 *pound fillets of sole or haddock*
1 *(8-ounce) can marinara sauce*
¼ *teaspoon thyme*
⅛ *teaspoon salt*

To serve 4 to 6
3 *tablespoons butter*
2 *onions, diced*
2 *green peppers, diced*
2 *pounds fillets of sole or haddock*
1 *(16-ounce) can marinara sauce*
½ *teaspoon thyme*
¼ *teaspoon salt*

Melt butter in a large skillet. Sauté onion and green pepper for several minutes. Arrange fish in the skillet. Pour marinara sauce over all. Sprinkle with thyme and salt. Cover and simmer for 10 minutes (simmer 20 minutes if fish is frozen solid), spooning sauce over the fish occasionally. Serve at once.

BROILED LOBSTER TAILS

For each serving
1 *large or 2 small lobster tails*
2 *tablespoons butter*
1 *teaspoon lemon juice*

With a sharp knife, cut down through the hard back shell of each lobster tail and through the meat without cutting the bony membrane of the undershell. Spread open, exposing the lobster meat. Melt butter and add lemon juice to it. Brush part of this mixture over the exposed lobster meat. Broil for about 10 minutes. Avoid overcooking as lobster meat will toughen. Serve remaining butter–lemon juice in individual sauce cups. Serve at once.

LOBSTER THERMIDOR

To serve 3	To serve 6
3 lobster tails, cooked	6 lobster tails, cooked
3 tablespoons butter	6 tablespoons butter
2 tablespoons flour	¼ cup flour
1 cup light cream	2 cups light cream
¼ teaspoon salt	½ teaspoon salt
⅛ teaspoon nutmeg	¼ teaspoon nutmeg
1 tablespoon sherry	2 tablespoons sherry
2 tablespoons grated cheddar cheese	¼ cup grated cheddar cheese
Paprika	Paprika

Remove meat from lobster tails and cut into bite-sized chunks. In a saucepan, melt butter. Add flour. Stir in cream. Add salt, nutmeg, and sherry. Add lobster chunks. Cook until thick. Fill lobster shells with the mixture. Sprinkle 2 teaspoons of grated cheddar cheese on top of each filled shell. Sprinkle with paprika. Place under the broiler until cheese is melted. Serve at once.

SHRIMP CREOLE

To serve 2 or 3	To serve 4 to 6
1 onion, sliced	2 onions, sliced
2 stalks celery, diced	4 stalks celery, diced
1 clove garlic, peeled and minced	1 or 2 cloves garlic, peeled and minced
2 tablespoons olive oil	3 tablespoons olive oil
2 teaspoons flour	1 tablespoon flour
½ teaspoon salt	1 teaspoon salt
½ teaspoon sugar	1 teaspoon sugar
2 teaspoons chili powder	1 tablespoon chili powder
⅔ cup water	1 cup water
1 cup whole canned tomatoes	2 cups whole canned tomatoes
1 cup peas, fresh or frozen	2 cups peas, fresh or frozen
2 teaspoons vinegar	1 tablespoon vinegar
1 cup shrimp, cleaned and peeled	2 cups shrimp, cleaned and peeled

In a 2-quart saucepan, sauté the onions, celery, and garlic in the heated oil for about 10 minutes. Stir flour, salt, sugar, and chili into the water; then add mixture to the saucepan. Simmer over low heat, uncovered, for 15 minutes. Add tomatoes, peas, vinegar, and shrimp. Simmer an additional 15 minutes. Do not overcook as shrimp may get tough. This recipe can be prepared in advance and reheated just before serving.

SHRIMP NEWBURG

A QUICK-TRICK WAY

To serve 2 or 3	*To serve 4 to 6*
2 tablespoons butter	3 tablespoons butter
¼ pound mushrooms, sliced	½ pound mushrooms, sliced
1 pound shrimp, peeled and cleaned	2 pounds shrimp, peeled and cleaned
1 (10-ounce) can frozen shrimp soup	2 (10-ounce) cans frozen shrimp soup
½ (10½-ounce) can condensed mushroom soup	1 (10½-ounce) can condensed mushroom soup
¼ cup light cream	½ cup light cream
2 tablespoons sherry	¼ cup sherry
1 teaspoon dry mustard	2 teaspoons dry mustard
⅛ teaspoon salt	¼ teaspoon salt
Dash of pepper	⅛ teaspoon pepper
2 tablespoons grated Parmesan cheese	¼ cup grated Parmesan cheese

In a skillet, melt butter; add sliced mushrooms and sauté until golden brown. Scrape mushrooms and butter into a casserole. Add shrimp. In a separate bowl, combine thawed shrimp soup, mushroom soup, cream, sherry, mustard, salt, and pepper. Pour this mixture over the shrimp. Sprinkle the top with grated Parmesan cheese. Bake in a 350-degree oven for about 30 minutes. This recipe can be prepared in advance, refrigerated, and baked just before serving.

ISLAND FRIED SHRIMP

To serve 2 or 3

1 *(1-pound) package frozen
    breaded butterfly shrimp*

1 *egg*

½ *cup coconut flakes*

¼ *cup flour*

½ *cup oil*

Duck sauce (optional)

To serve 4 to 6

2 *(1-pound) packages frozen
    breaded butterfly shrimp*

2 *eggs*

1 *cup coconut flakes*

½ *cup flour*

1 *cup oil*

Duck sauce (optional)

Remove breaded butterfly shrimp from package while still frozen. Beat egg. Combine coconut and flour in a separate bowl. Dip each shrimp into the egg, and then roll it in the coconut–flour mixture. Heat oil in a skillet; when bubbling, arrange shrimp in it and carefully brown on all sides. Remove fried shrimp to drain on paper towels. Serve immediately with a bottled duck sauce if desired.

HOT CRAB MEAT ON HERBED CROUTONS

A QUICK-TRICK WAY

To serve 2 or 4

½ *cup olive oil*

2 *tablespoons onion flakes*

2 *tablespoons dried parsley*

2 *cloves garlic, peeled and crushed*

2 *(7-ounce) cans crab meat, cut up*

1 *cup packaged herbed croutons*

Heat oil in a skillet. Add onion flakes, parsley, and crushed garlic. Add cut-up crab meat and sauté gently, turning pieces to coat with onion, parsley, and garlic. Serve at once, spooned over herbed croutons, as an appetizer. Serves 2 if used as a main course, 4 as an appetizer.

SCALLOP KABOBS

To serve 4 to 6

1 *pound scallops, fresh or frozen*
1 *(13½-ounce) can pineapple chunks, drained*
1 *(4-ounce) can button mushrooms, drained*
1 *green pepper, cut into 1-inch squares*
¼ *cup melted butter*
¼ *cup lemon juice*
¼ *cup chopped parsley*
¼ *cup soy sauce*
½ *teaspoon salt*
Dash of pepper
12 *slices bacon*

If scallops are frozen, allow them to thaw before using. Rinse scallops with cold water to remove any shell particles. Place pineapple, mushrooms, green pepper, and scallops in a bowl. Combine butter, lemon juice, parsley, soy sauce, salt, and pepper. Pour sauce over scallop mixture and let stand for 30 minutes, stirring occasionally. Fry bacon until cooked but not crisp. Cut each slice in half. Using long skewers, alternate scallops, pineapple, mushrooms, green pepper, and bacon until skewers are filled. Broil about 4 inches from heat for 5 minutes on each side, basting with sauce. When bacon is crisp, serve at once.

❧ 10 ❧

All About Meat

WHAT PROCUREMENT AGENT FOR A LARGE COMPANY WOULD DARE to make a purchase without making a careful study of the product? Housewives do not generally get fired for lack of knowledge, but they may waste thousands of dollars over the years in meat purchases unless they have taken the time to learn something about what they are paying for and why. A familiarity with the different cuts of meat and their uses will help you to plan your menus wisely and to purchase your meat knowledgeably. The meat charts on the following pages will start you on your way.

Let us take beef as an example. A beef carcass usually weighs over five hundred pounds and is roughly divided into eight major parts. The carcass is divided down the middle from front to back and becomes two sides of beef. Further division once across (between the twelfth and thirteenth ribs) creates two forequarters and two hindquarters. Naturally, the cuts of meat on one side are duplicated on the other, so you have to learn the butcher-cuts of only one half of the carcass.

The carcass also provides:

Beef liver	Tongue
Beef heart	Kidneys
Brains	Oxtail

What should you look for in judging beef? Quality beef is generally bright red in color; the flesh is firm, fine-grained, and well marbled with white fat. Meat is graded:

U.S. Prime	U.S. Commercial
U.S. Choice	U.S. Utility
U.S. Good	U.S. Cutter
U.S. Standard	U.S. Canner

The first three categories are preferred for home use; the better the quality of the meat, the better will be the taste. When evaluating a cut of meat, look at the trimming to determine whether you will have to pay a premium price for more fat than necessary. U.S. Choice, the grade that is most available at neighborhood markets, has less fat in the marbled graining and is generally more tender than U.S. Good grade.

What cuts of beef should you choose for good value and for good eating? Keep in mind that a low price may not always be a bargain. The more bone and the more fat a cut of meat has, the less the percentage of actual meat to be eaten. A good portion of meat for one person is one-third pound for boneless meat, one-half pound for meat with a small amount of bone, and one pound per person for very bony cuts such as spareribs.

The most expensive and tenderest cuts of meat come from the loin, rib, and sirloin sections of the animal. These cuts can be roasted in the oven or broiled. Other cuts such as round steaks and chuck roasts are less tender and usually must be pot-roasted, braised, or panfried.

All meat is perishable and it is important to store it properly. Fresh meat should be loosely wrapped and stored in the refrigerator. It may be kept safely for several days before using. Ground meat should be used within a day or two. Cured and smoked meats should be stored in the refrigerator in their original wrappings. Sausages and ready-to-serve meats should also be left in their original wrappings and refrigerated. Perishable canned meats should be stored in the refrigerator, unless the package states otherwise; they are not intended to be frozen. Frozen meat should be wrapped airtight with proper freezer materials and placed in the freezer immediately after purchase.

Leftover cooked meats should be refrigerated, covered, as soon as possible. Cool leftovers quickly; do not let them stay at room temperature, which will encourage the rapid multiplication of bacteria. If you are freezing leftover cooked meat, use a covering of gravy even if you have to thin the gravy with water to get the necessary amount. This will guarantee that the meat will be moist when the frozen leftovers are reheated.

Selecting, cooking, and storing meat requires a knowledgeable gal who cares about getting her money's worth. However, all your efforts will be in vain if you do not know how to carve meat properly as well as to serve it attractively. What good is cooking a roast to perfection if it ends up in a clumsy heap on the platter? This is an example of where togetherness really counts—your husband is the one who should master the art of carving while you can supply the diagrams and instructions that will show him how it is done. In this chapter I have included helpful illustrative material for carving the most popular meats. Study the material and then pass it on to your spouse.

There are four things to remember before the carver can begin his work:

1. Cook the meat properly. If a roast is cooked at too high an oven temperature, it may have a tough outer crust. If it is overcooked it will fall apart, no matter how skillful the carver.
2. Let the meat set for 15 to 20 minutes after it is removed from the oven, if it is a large roast. It will firm up and be easier to carve. Keep it in a warm place like the top of the range, and cover it lightly with a clean kitchen towel.
3. Remove all strings and skewers in the kitchen before the roast is to be carved. Don't give the carver this chore at the table. If it is a rolled roast you may leave on one or two strings to hold it together.
4. Make sure the carving knife is of good quality and is *sharp*.

Meat
Charts
and
Carving
Instructions

Beef Chart

Retail Cuts of Beef—Where They Come From and How To Cook Them

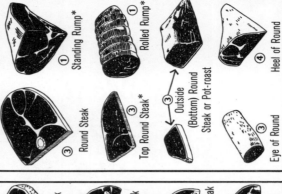
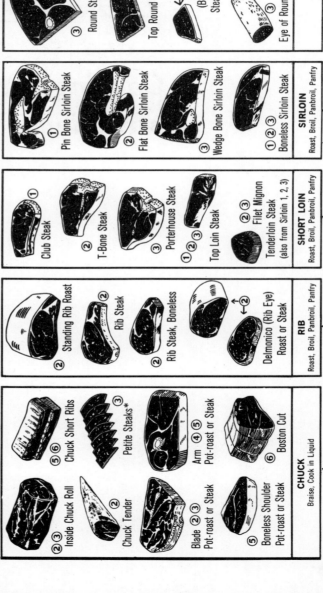

ROUND
Braise, Cook in Liquid

① Standing Rump*
① Rolled Rump*
③ Round Steak
③ Top Round Steak*
③ Outside (Bottom) Round Steak or Pot-roast
④ Heel of Round
③ Eye of Round

SIRLOIN
Roast, Broil, Panbroil, Panfry

① Pin Bone Sirloin Steak
② Flat Bone Sirloin Steak
③ Wedge Bone Sirloin Steak
① ② ③ Boneless Sirloin Steak

SHORT LOIN
Roast, Broil, Panbroil, Panfry

① Club Steak
② T-Bone Steak
③ Porterhouse Steak
① ② ③ Top Loin Steak
② ③ Filet Mignon Tenderloin Steak (also from Sirloin 1, 2, 3)

RIB
Roast, Broil, Panbroil, Panfry

② Standing Rib Roast
② Rib Steak
② Rib Steak, Boneless
② Delmonico (Rib Eye) Roast or Steak

CHUCK
Braise, Cook in Liquid

⑤ ⑥ Chuck Short Ribs
③ Petite Steaks*
④ ⑤ Arm Pot-roast or Steak
⑥ Boston Cut
② ③ Inside Chuck Roll
② Chuck Tender
② ③ Blade Pot-roast or Steak
⑤ Boneless Shoulder Pot-roast or Steak

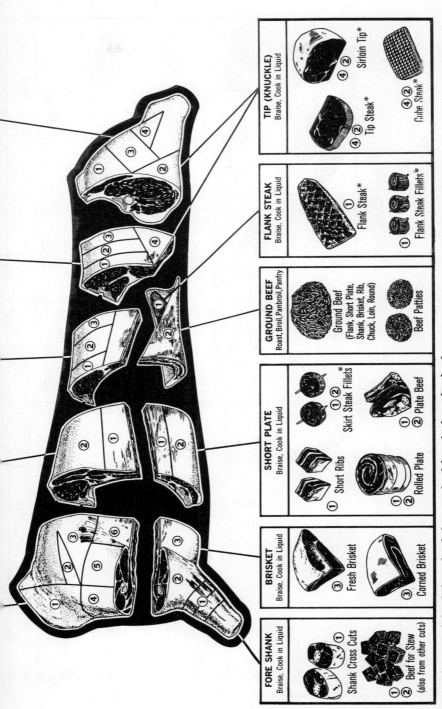

TIP (KNUCKLE)
Braise, Cook in Liquid

④ ② Sirloin Tip*

④ ② Tip Steak*

④ ② Cube Steak*

FLANK STEAK
Braise, Cook in Liquid

① Flank Steak*

① Flank Steak Fillets*

GROUND BEEF
Roast, Broil, Panbroil, Panfry

Ground Beef (Flank, Short Plate, Shank, Brisket, Rib, Chuck, Loin, Round)

Beef Patties

SHORT PLATE
Braise, Cook in Liquid

① ② Skirt Steak Fillets*

① Short Ribs

① ② Rolled Plate

① ② Plate Beef

BRISKET
Braise, Cook in Liquid

③ Fresh Brisket

③ Corned Brisket

FORE SHANK
Braise, Cook in Liquid

① Shank Cross Cuts

① ② Beef for Stew (also from other cuts)

* May be roasted, broiled, panbroiled, or panfried from high-quality beef

Veal Chart

Retail Cuts of Veal—Where They Come From and How To Cook Them

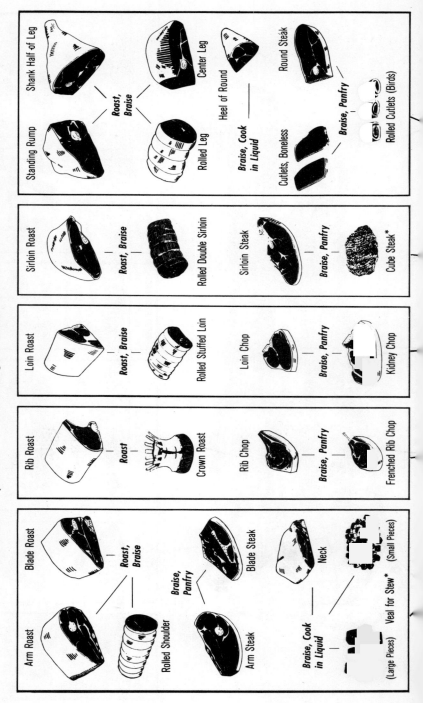

64

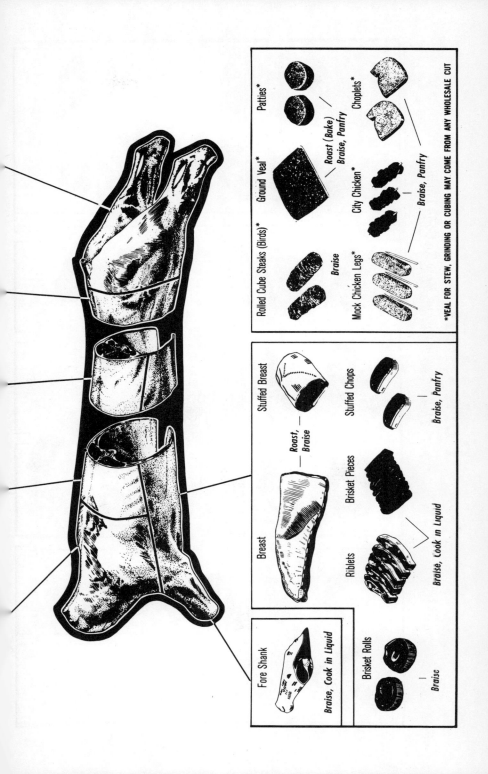

Patties*

Roast (Bake),
Braise, Panfry

Ground Veal*

Choplets*

Braise, Panfry

City Chicken*

Rolled Cube Steaks (Birds)*

Braise

Mock Chicken Legs*

*VEAL FOR STEW, GRINDING OR CUBING MAY COME FROM ANY WHOLESALE CUT

Stuffed Breast

Roast,
Braise

Stuffed Chops

Braise, Panfry

Breast

Brisket Pieces

Riblets

Braise, Cook in Liquid

Fore Shank

Braise, Cook in Liquid

Brisket Rolls

Braise

Pork Chart

Retail Cuts of Pork—Where They Come From and How To Cook Them

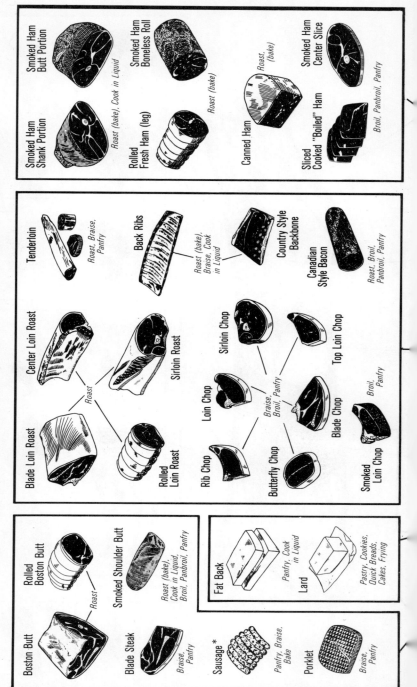

Smoked Ham Butt Portion

Smoked Ham Boneless Roll

Canned Ham
Roast,
(bake)

Smoked Ham Center Slice
Broil, Panbroil, Panfry

Smoked Ham Shank Portion
Roast (bake), Cook in Liquid

Rolled Fresh Ham (leg)
Roast (bake)

Sliced Cooked "Boiled" Ham
Broil, Panbroil, Panfry

Tenderloin
Roast, Braise, Panfry

Back Ribs
Roast (bake), Braise, Cook in Liquid

Country Style Backbone

Canadian Style Bacon
Roast, Broil, Panbroil, Panfry

Center Loin Roast

Sirloin Roast

Sirloin Chop

Top Loin Chop
Broil, Panfry

Blade Loin Roast
Roast

Rolled Loin Roast

Loin Chop

Rib Chop

Butterfly Chop
Braise, Broil, Panfry

Blade Chop

Smoked Loin Chop

Boston Butt

Rolled Boston Butt
Roast

Smoked Shoulder Butt
Roast (bake), Cook in Liquid, Broil, Panbroil, Panfry

Blade Steak
Braise, Panfry

Sausage*
Panfry, Braise, Bake

Porklet
Braise, Panfry

Fat Back
Panfry, Cook in Liquid

Lard
Pastry, Cookies, Quick Breads, Cakes, Frying

Spareribs

Roast (bake), Braise, Cook in Liquid

Slab Bacon

Broil, Panbroil, Panfry, Bake

Salt Pork

Broil, Panbroil, Panfry, Cook in Liquid, Bake

Sliced Bacon

Smoked Picnic

Roast (bake), Cook in Liquid

Canned Picnic

Roast, (bake)

Fresh Picnic

Roast

Rolled Fresh Picnic

Roast

Arm Roast

Roast

Arm Steak

Braise, Panfry

Smoked Hock

Cook in Liquid

Fresh Hock

Braise

Canned Luncheon Meat*

Roast (bake), Broil, Panbroil

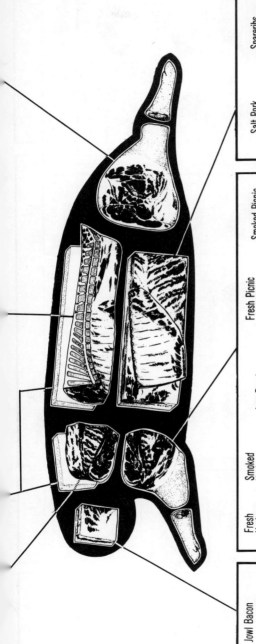

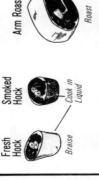

Jowl Bacon

Cook in Liquid, Broil, Panbroil, Panfry

Pig's Feet

Cook in Liquid, Braise

*These items may come from several areas of the pork side

Lamb Chart

Retail Cuts of Lamb—Where They Come From and How To Cook Them

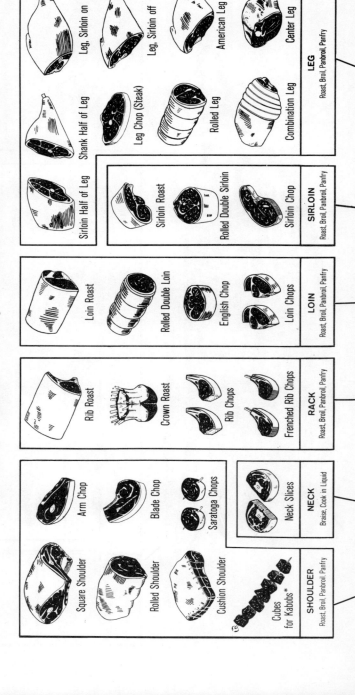

LEG
Roast, Broil, Panbroil, Panfry

Leg, Sirloin on
Leg, Sirloin off
American Leg
Center Leg
Shank Half of Leg
Leg Chop (Steak)
Rolled Leg
Combination Leg
Sirloin Half of Leg

SIRLOIN
Roast, Broil, Panbroil, Panfry

Sirloin Roast
Rolled Double Sirloin
Sirloin Chop

LOIN
Roast, Broil, Panbroil, Panfry

Loin Roast
Rolled Double Loin
English Chop
Loin Chops

RACK
Roast, Broil, Panbroil, Panfry

Rib Roast
Crown Roast
Rib Chops
Frenched Rib Chops

NECK
Braise, Cook in Liquid

Neck Slices

SHOULDER
Roast, Broil, Panbroil, Panfry

Arm Chop
Blade Chop
Saratoga Chops
Square Shoulder
Rolled Shoulder
Cushion Shoulder
Cubes for Kabobs*

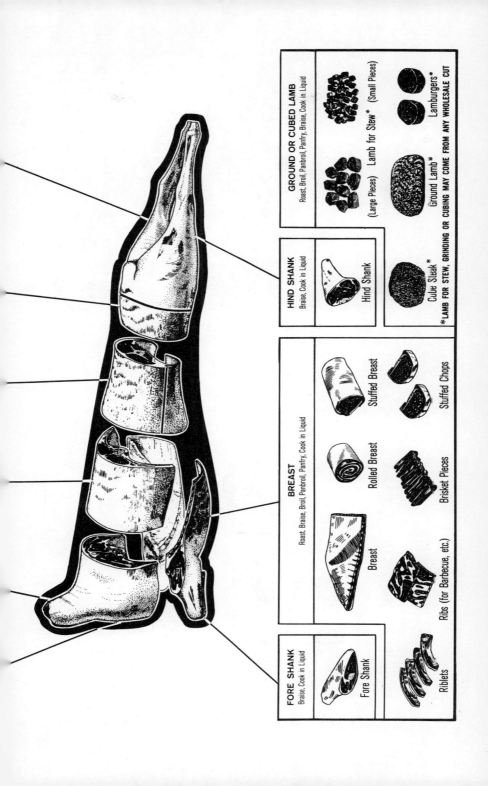

GROUND OR CUBED LAMB
Roast, Broil, Panbroil, Panfry, Braise, Cook in Liquid

(Large Pieces) Lamb for Stew* (Small Pieces)

Ground Lamb*   Lamburgers*

Cube Steak*

*LAMB FOR STEW, GRINDING OR CUBING MAY COME FROM ANY WHOLESALE CUT

HIND SHANK
Braise, Cook in Liquid

Hind Shank

BREAST
Roast, Braise, Broil, Panbroil, Panfry, Cook in Liquid

Breast   Rolled Breast   Stuffed Breast

Brisket Pieces   Stuffed Chops

Ribs (for Barbecue, etc.)

FORE SHANK
Braise, Cook in Liquid

Fore Shank

Riblets

BEEF DELMONICO (RIB EYE) ROAST

Hold roast firmly with fork while carving cross-grain slices of desired thickness.

BEEF STANDING RIB ROAST

When necessary, remove wedge-shaped slice from large end so roast will stand firmly on this end. Insert fork below top rib. Carve across the face of roast to the rib bone.

Cut along rib bone with tip of knife to release slice. Slide knife back under slice and, steadying it with fork, lift slice to side of platter or auxiliary platter.

BEEF BLADE POT ROAST

Cut between muscles and around bones to remove one solid section of pot roast at a time.

Turn removed section so meat fibers are parallel to platter. This makes it possible to carve across the grain of meat.

Holding meat with fork, carve slices about one-quarter-inch thick.

ROLLED ROASTS

Most rolled roasts are carved in the same manner as the beef rolled rump shown here. The exception is a beef rolled rib roast which is usually stood on end and carved like the beef standing rib roast shown on page 70.

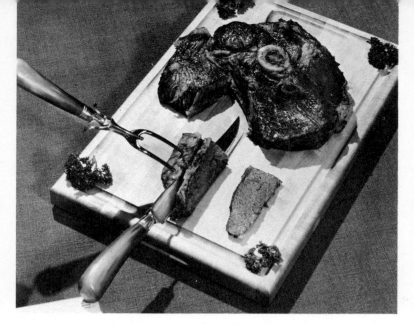

ARM ROASTS AND POT ROASTS

Pork and veal arm roasts are carved in the same way as the beef arm pot roasts shown here. The object is to separate solid pieces of meat at natural dividing seams. Turn each piece on its side and cut cross-grain slices of the desired thickness.

BEEF PORTERHOUSE STEAK

Hold steak steady with fork. Use tip of knife to cut closely around bone. Lift bone to one side of platter.

Carve across full width of steak, cutting through both top loin and tenderloin. Diagonal slicing, instead of perpendicular, is recommended for thick steaks.

PORK LOIN ROAST

Before roast is brought to table, remove back bone, leaving as little meat on it as possible. Place roast on platter with rib side facing carver so he can see angle of ribs and make his slices accordingly.

Insert fork in top of roast. Make slices by cutting closely along each side of rib bone. One slice will contain the rib; the next will be boneless.

WHOLE HAM

Ham is placed on platter with decorated or fat side up and shank to carver's right. Location of bones in right and left hams may be confusing; double-check location of knee cap which may be on near or far side of ham. Remove two or three lengthwise slices from thin side of ham which contains knee cap.

Make perpendicular slices down to leg bone. Release slices by cutting along leg bone.

SHANK HALF OF HAM

With shank at carver's left, turn ham so thick cushion side is up. Cut along top of leg and shank bones and under fork to lift off boneless cushion.

Place cushion meat on carving board and make perpendicular slices. Cut around leg bone with tip of knife to remove meat from this bone. Turn meat so that thickest side is down. Slice in the same manner as the cushion piece.

BUTT HALF OF HAM

Place butt half of ham on platter with "face" or center on carving board. Cut down along bone to remove boneless piece from side of ham. The boneless piece may be on the near or far side, depending on whether it is from right or left leg.

With boneless piece resting on freshly cut surface, carve into desired cross-grain servings.

Hold remaining piece with fork and carve across meat until knife strikes bone. Release each slice from bone with tip of knife and lift it to side of platter.

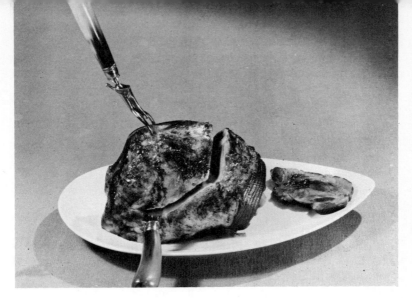

PICNIC SHOULDER

Carving is the same for both a roasted smoked picnic and a roasted fresh picnic. Remove lengthwise slice, and turn picnic so that it rests on the surface just cut.

Cut down to arm bone at a point near elbow bone. Turn knife and cut along arm bone to remove boneless arm meat. Carve boneless arm meat by making perpendicular slices from top of meat down to cutting board.

Remove meat from each side of arm bone. Carve the two boneless pieces.

LAMB LEG ROAST

With lower leg bone to carver's right, remove two or three lengthwise slices from thin side of leg. This side has the knee cap.

Turn roast up on its base. Starting where shank joins the leg bone loosen slices by cutting under them, following closely along top of leg bone. Lift slices to platter for serving.

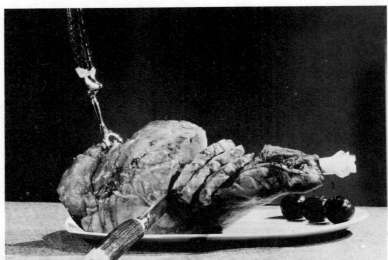

SLICED STEAK WITH BURGUNDY–MUSHROOM GRAVY

To serve 2 or 3

1½-pound sirloin steak
¼ teaspoon salt
⅛ teaspoon pepper
1 teaspoon prepared
    mustard
Burgundy–Mushroom Gravy
    (see page 132)

To serve 4 to 6

3-pound sirloin steak
½ teaspoon salt
¼ teaspoon pepper
1½ teaspoons prepared
    mustard
Burgundy–Mushroom Gravy
    (see page 132)

Season sirloin steak with salt and pepper. Spread the top surface with prepared mustard. Broil 5 minutes, then turn steak over and broil an additional 5 minutes, or until desired degree of doneness is achieved. Remove to a platter and pour Burgundy–Mushroom Gravy over the top. Slice and serve at once.

LONDON BROIL

To serve 2 or 3

1 (1-pound) flank steak
¼ teaspoon meat tenderizer
¼ teaspoon garlic salt
⅛ teaspoon ground black
    pepper
1 tablespoon salad oil
1 teaspoon lemon juice

To serve 4 to 6

1 (2-pound) flank steak
½ teaspoon meat tenderizer
½ teaspoon garlic salt
¼ teaspoon ground black
    pepper
2 tablespoons salad oil
2 teaspoons lemon juice

Sprinkle flank steak with meat tenderizer, pierce with the tines of a fork, and let stand at room temperature for 10 minutes. Combine garlic salt, pepper, salad oil, and lemon juice. Place steak on a broiler rack. Brush steak with half the oil mixture. Broil for 4 to 5 minutes. Turn and brush with remaining oil mixture; broil 4 minutes longer, or until meat is done to your taste. Carve meat into thin slices on an extreme diagonal across the grain. Serve at once.

SAUERBRATEN

To serve 2 or 3
2½ - to 3-*pound top round
    beef roast*
1 *cup vinegar*
½ *cup water*
1½ *teaspoons sugar*
2 *cloves*
1 *bay leaf*
3 *whole peppercorns*
1 *onion, sliced*
2 *tablespoons flour*
2 *tablespoons olive oil*
4 *gingersnap cookies*

To serve 4 to 6
3½ - to 4-*pound top round
    beef roast*
2 *cups vinegar*
1 *cup water*
1 *tablespoon sugar*
4 *cloves*
2 *bay leaves*
6 *whole peppercorns*
2 *onions, sliced*
3 *tablespoons flour*
¼ *cup olive oil*
8 *gingersnap cookies*

Place a large plastic bag in a deep bowl; insert beef roast standing on end. In a saucepan, heat vinegar, water, sugar, cloves, bay leaf, peppercorns, and sliced onion for 5 minutes. Cool. Pour marinade into plastic bag over meat and fasten with a wire closure. Refrigerate for 2 days, turning the bag occasionally to redistribute the marinade. When ready to cook, remove meat and wipe it dry. Pat meat with flour. Heat oil in a heavy saucepan or Dutch oven; brown meat on all sides over high heat. Reduce heat, add remaining marinade, and simmer until meat is tender to the insertion of a fork, approximately 1½ to 2 hours. Crumble gingersnaps and add to gravy, heating until gravy thickens. Serve in slices with gravy.

SAVORY BRISKET OF BEEF

A QUICK-TRICK WAY

To serve 4 to 6
1 *first-cut brisket of beef (about 4 pounds)*
1 *package dehydrated onion soup mix*
½ *teaspoon paprika*
1 *cup water*

Place brisket of beef in a Dutch oven or a roasting pan. Empty entire package of onion soup mix over the roast. Sprinkle with paprika. Pour water around the roast. Cover with lid of Dutch oven or with foil. Place in a 325-degree oven for 2 hours. When you remove the cover you should have a nice onion gravy ready to be ladled over the brisket slices. The meat will be tender, well done like pot roast, and delicious.

CORNED BEEF AND CABBAGE

To serve 2 or 3	*To serve 4 to 6*
1 *(3-pound) corned beef brisket*	1 *(5-pound) corned beef brisket*
1 *onion, sliced*	2 *onions, sliced*
2 *carrots, pared and quartered*	4 *carrots, pared and quartered*
3 *peppercorns*	5 *peppercorns*
1 *bay leaf*	2 *bay leaves*
1 *small head cabbage*	1 *large head cabbage*
3 *potatoes, peeled and quartered*	6 *potatoes, peeled and quartered*

Place corned beef in a deep pot; cover with cold water. Add onion, carrots, peppercorns, and bay leaf. Bring to a boil, cover, and simmer gently for at least 30 minutes per pound. Then cut cabbage into quarters and add to pot; add potatoes. Simmer for 25 minutes more, or until tender. Serve with mustard.

BEEF STROGANOFF

To serve 2 or 3	*To serve 4 to 6*
1 *pound round steak*	2 *pounds round steak*
2 *tablespoons olive oil*	3 *tablespoons olive oil*
½ *pound fresh mushrooms*	1 *pound fresh mushrooms*
1 *tablespoon butter*	2 *tablespoons butter*
1 *onion, sliced thin*	2 *onions, sliced thin*
1 *tablespoon flour*	2 *tablespoons flour*
½ *teaspoon paprika*	1 *teaspoon paprika*
¼ *teaspoon dry mustard*	½ *teaspoon dry mustard*
¼ *teaspoon salt*	½ *teaspoon salt*
⅛ *teaspoon pepper*	¼ *teaspoon pepper*
¼ *cup white wine*	½ *cup white wine*
1 *cup dairy sour cream*	2 *cups dairy sour cream*

Cut steak into 1-inch cubes. Heat oil in a skillet. Brown steak in hot oil, cover, and simmer for 5 minutes. Slice mushrooms thick and add to steak; cover and simmer for 10 minutes more. Remove steak and mushrooms to the top of a large double boiler. Melt butter in the same skillet; add onion slices and sauté until limp. Sprinkle with flour, paprika, mustard, salt, and pepper; stir well and brown these ingredients together. Then pour white wine in slowly, stirring constantly. Remove from heat and stir in sour cream just before serving. Pour mixture over steak and mushrooms and heat thoroughly over hot water. Do not allow mixture to boil. Serve at once, or transfer to a chafing dish and steam over hot water.

BEEF BOURGUIGNONNE

To serve 2 or 3	*To serve 4 to 6*
1 *pound boned, lean beef chuck, cut in cubes*	2 *pounds boned, lean beef chuck, cut in cubes*
½ *cup flour*	1 *cup flour*
½ *teaspoon garlic powder*	1 *teaspoon garlic powder*
½ *teaspoon paprika*	1 *teaspoon paprika*
¼ *teaspoon salt*	½ *teaspoon salt*
2 *tablespoons olive oil*	3 *tablespoons olive oil*
½ *cup Burgundy wine*	1 *cup Burgundy wine*
6 *tiny whole white onions*	12 *tiny whole white onions*
1 *cup beef bouillon*	2 *cups beef bouillon*
1 *tablespoon tomato paste*	2 *tablespoons tomato paste*
1 *bay leaf*	2 *bay leaves*
½ *teaspoon salt*	1 *teaspoon salt*
¼ *teaspoon thyme*	½ *teaspoon thyme*
3 *carrots, peeled*	6 *carrots, peeled*
3 *potatoes, peeled*	6 *potatoes, peeled*
¼ *pound mushrooms, sliced*	½ *pound mushrooms, sliced*

Dredge beef cubes in a mixture of flour, garlic powder, paprika, and salt. Brown lightly in oil in the bottom of a Dutch oven.

Pour Burgundy wine over beef. Arrange onions around the beef. Pour bouillon mixed with tomato paste over beef. Add bay leaf, salt, and thyme. Cover and bake in a 325-degree oven for 1½ to 2 hours. Add carrots, potatoes, and mushrooms. Cover and bake an additional ½ hour, or until vegetables are tender.

MEAT BALLS

To serve 2 or 3	To serve 4 to 6
1 pound chopped beef	2 pounds chopped beef
¼ cup water	½ cup water
2 slices bread	4 slices bread
1 egg	2 eggs
1 small onion, grated	1 large onion, grated
¼ teaspoon salt	½ teaspoon salt
⅛ teaspoon pepper	¼ teaspoon pepper
¼ teaspoon powdered garlic	½ teaspoon powdered garlic
1 tablespoon chopped parsley	2 tablespoons chopped parsley
1 tablespoon grated Parmesan cheese	2 tablespoons grated Parmesan cheese
1 onion, sliced	2 onions, sliced
¼ cup olive oil	½ cup olive oil
1 (1-pound) can Italian tomatoes, packed in puree	1 (2-pound) can Italian tomatoes, packed in puree
¼ teaspoon oregano	½ teaspoon oregano

Place meat in a bowl. In a separate dish, pour water over bread and let it soak in. Shred bread as you put it in bowl with meat. Break egg over meat. Add grated onion, salt, pepper, garlic, parsley, and Parmesan cheese. Work all through evenly with your clean hands. Sauté sliced onion in olive oil in a large saucepan. Form small meat balls by rolling about a heaping teaspoonful of the meat mixture between the palms of your hands. Using low heat, place them in the saucepan as you roll them, browning the meat balls on all sides. When all are browned, add tomatoes and oregano. Cover and simmer, stirring occasionally, for 45 minutes.

FLUFFY MEAT LOAF

A QUICK-TRICK WAY

To serve 2 or 3
1 *pound chopped beef*
½ *package dehydrated onion soup mix*
¼ *cup tomato juice*
2 *tablespoons instant potato mix*

To serve 4 to 6
2 *pounds chopped beef*
1 *package dehydrated onion soup mix*
½ *cup tomato juice*
¼ *cup instant potato mix*

Combine chopped beef, onion soup mix, tomato juice, and instant potato mix. Mix ingredients together well. Pat mixture into a lightly greased loaf pan and place in a 350-degree oven for 40 to 60 minutes, depending on quantity of beef used. Remove from oven and serve hot slices.

CHEESEBURGER HERO SANDWICH

To make 8 slices
2 *pounds lean ground beef*
1 *(8-ounce) can tomato sauce*
½ *teaspoon salt*
¼ *teaspoon pepper*
½ *cup onion, grated*
¼ *cup chopped parsley*
¼ *cup fine bread crumbs*
1 *long loaf French bread*
6 *slices American cheese*

Combine beef with tomato sauce. Add salt, pepper, grated onion, chopped parsley, and bread crumbs. Cut bread in half lengthwise. Spread half of the beef mixture on each half loaf. Bake on an ungreased cookie sheet at 400 degrees for 20 minutes, or until well browned. Remove from oven. Pile American cheese slices on top of each other and cut in fourths. Arrange these small squares of cheese, overlapping the points, down the center of the length of the bread. Return to oven and bake for several minutes longer until cheese is partially melted. Make 3 diagonal cuts across each half loaf and serve at once.

VEAL SCALOPPINE

To serve 2 or 3
¾ pound thin veal slices
½ teaspoon salt
¼ teaspoon pepper
1 tablespoon flour
¼ cup olive oil
¼ pound mushrooms, sliced
½ cup white wine
Lemon slices

To serve 4 to 6
1½ pounds thin veal slices
1 teaspoon salt
½ teaspoon pepper
2 tablespoons flour
½ cup olive oil
½ pound mushrooms, sliced
¾ cup white wine
Lemon slices

Have butcher flatten veal slices for you, or do it yourself with a wooden meat mallet. Combine salt, pepper, and flour. Dredge veal in this mixture until all sides are coated lightly. Heat oil in a skillet. Brown veal slices on both sides, doing several slices at a time and removing each slice when it is browned to make room for the next slices. Remove last browned slices and sauté sliced mushrooms in remaining oil. Return the meat to the skillet with mushrooms. Pour white wine over all and cook for several minutes. Remove meat to a platter and pour the sauce and mushrooms over the veal. Garnish with thin, fresh lemon slices. Serve at once.

VEAL CUTLET CORDON BLEU

To serve 2 or 3
6 thin veal cutlets
3 slices Swiss cheese
3 thin slices cooked ham
½ cup flour
1 egg
¼ teaspoon prepared mustard
1 tablespoon milk
¼ teaspoon salt
½ cup bread crumbs
¼ cup olive oil
Lemon slices

To serve 4 to 6
12 thin veal cutlets
6 slices Swiss cheese
6 thin slices cooked ham
1 cup flour
2 eggs
½ teaspoon prepared mustard
2 tablespoons milk
½ teaspoon salt
1 cup bread crumbs
½ cup olive oil
Lemon slices

82

Have your butcher pound the veal cutlets flat or do it yourself. On half of the cutlets, place a slice of Swiss cheese and then a slice of ham; top with a second cutlet. Press edges closed. Dip each cutlet sandwich in flour, coating well. Beat egg slightly; add mustard, milk, and salt. Dip each floured cutlet into egg mixture and then into bread crumbs. Heat olive oil in a skillet and fry cutlets until golden brown on both sides. Serve garnished with a slice of fresh lemon.

VEAL CHOPS IN MUSHROOM SAUCE

To serve 2 or 3	*To serve 4 to 6*
2 tablespoons butter	¼ cup butter
¼ pound fresh mushrooms, sliced	½ pound fresh mushrooms, sliced
1 can tomato sauce	2 cans tomato sauce
1 tablespoon grated Parmesan cheese	2 tablespoons grated Parmesan cheese
1 tablespoon chopped parsley	2 tablespoons chopped parsley
1 tablespoon sherry	2 tablespoons sherry
1 teaspoon lemon juice	2 teaspoons lemon juice
4 loin or rib veal chops	8 loin or rib veal chops
1 egg, beaten	2 eggs, beaten
¼ cup bread crumbs	½ cup bread crumbs
¼ cup olive oil	½ cup olive oil

Melt butter in a small saucepan; add sliced mushrooms and cook over low heat for several minutes until mushrooms are limp. Add tomato sauce, Parmesan cheese, parsley, sherry, and lemon juice. Cover and allow to simmer while you fry the veal chops. Dip each veal chop first into the beaten egg and then into the bread crumbs, coating well. Heat oil in a large skillet; brown chops on both sides, then pour hot sauce over the chops in the skillet. Cover and simmer for 20 minutes. This recipe can be prepared in advance. Place browned chops in a flat baking pan, cover with sauce, and then refrigerate; to heat, bake in a 350-degree oven for 30 minutes just before serving.

ORIENTAL VEAL ROAST

To serve 2 or 3
½ cup pineapple juice
¼ cup soy sauce
¼ cup sherry
1 clove garlic, minced
1 teaspoon brown sugar
1 teaspoon dry mustard
½ teaspoon ginger
¼ teaspoon thyme
1 (2-pound) shoulder of veal
   roast, boned

To serve 4 to 6
1 cup pineapple juice
½ cup soy sauce
½ cup sherry
2 cloves garlic, minced
2 teaspoons brown sugar
2 teaspoons dry mustard
1 teaspoon ginger
½ teaspoon thyme
1 (4-pound) shoulder of veal
   roast, boned

Place a plastic bag in a deep bowl; pour pineapple juice, soy sauce, and sherry into bag. Add minced garlic, brown sugar, dry mustard, ginger, and thyme; stir to blend. Place boned and tied shoulder of veal roast into the bag; fasten top with a wire closure. Let stand for several hours at room temperature, or in refrigerator overnight, changing position of the bag often to redistribute the marinade. Remove roast and place in a pan; roast, uncovered, at 350 degrees for 30 minutes per pound of meat. Midway in the roasting, spoon remaining marinade over the meat. When done, slice and serve with gravy.

To make the gravy, add a small amount of boiling water to the liquid in the pan and scrape all the drippings into it.

APRICOT–HAM BAKE

To serve 2 or 3
1-pound center ham slice
½ (16-ounce) can apricot
   halves
¼ teaspoon dry mustard
1 tablespoon brown sugar
⅛ teaspoon ginger

To serve 4 to 6
2-pound center ham slice
1 (16-ounce) can apricot
   halves
½ teaspoon dry mustard
2 tablespoons brown sugar
¼ teaspoon ginger

Place ham slice in a flat baking dish. Top with apricot halves, reserving juice. To apricot juice, add dry mustard, brown sugar,

84

and ginger; stir until dry ingredients are dissolved. Pour over the ham slice; cover with regular pan cover or with foil. Bake for about 25 minutes per pound, in a 350-degree oven, basting occasionally. Serve hot with juice from pan.

PRUNE-STUFFED LOIN OF PORK

To serve 6 to 8
1 *pork loin (about 4 pounds)*
½ *teaspoon sage*
1 *teaspoon salt*
½ *teaspoon pepper*
2 *(1-pound) jars cooked prunes*
12 *small white onions*
2 *tablespoons cornstarch*
1 *tablespoon vinegar*
½ *cup bouillon or water*

Wipe pork loin with a damp towel. With sharp knife, separate the thickest part of the meat from the bone, without detaching bone, to form a pocket. Rub the roast with sage, salt, and pepper. Drain and reserve the liquid from the prunes. Remove and discard the pits. Stuff 24 prunes with half an onion each. Chop remaining prunes and reserve. Fill the pocket of the roast with stuffed prunes. Tie white string around the roast at several places to hold the stuffing. Arrange the meat on a rack in a roasting pan, and roast in a 350-degree oven for 2½ hours. Stir the cornstarch into a small amount of the reserved prune liquid, add remaining prune liquid, and cook over low heat, stirring until mixture is clear and thickened. Add reserved chopped prunes and vinegar and additional salt if needed. Baste the meat with some of this sauce frequently until it is very well done and tender. Remove meat to a platter and discard strings. Pour off the fat from the roasting pan; add bouillon to pan and cook for a few minutes, stirring in the browned bits that cling to the pan. Stir in remaining prune sauce. Serve with roast.

SHOULDER OF LAMB BRETONNE

To serve 2 or 3

1 (2-pound) shoulder of lamb
    roast
1 tablespoon butter
½ teaspoon salt
¼ teaspoon pepper
1 tablespoon olive oil
1 onion, sliced
1 clove garlic, minced
1 tablespoon chopped parsley
¼ teaspoon thyme
1 bay leaf
1 (1-pound) can tomatoes

To serve 4 to 6

1 (4-pound) shoulder of lamb
    roast
2 tablespoons butter
1 teaspoon salt
½ teaspoon pepper
2 tablespoons olive oil
2 onions, sliced
2 cloves garlic, minced
2 tablespoons chopped parsley
½ teaspoon thyme
2 bay leaves
2 (1-pound) cans tomatoes

Have shoulder of lamb boned, rolled, and tied by your butcher. Place lamb roast in a roasting pan; spread roast with butter and season with salt and pepper. Place in a 325-degree oven for 30 minutes per pound. Meanwhile, heat olive oil in a skillet; add sliced onions, minced garlic, parsley, and thyme. Simmer for 10 minutes. Add bay leaf and tomatoes and simmer for an additional 20 minutes, stirring occasionally. Spoon tomato mixture over and around lamb roast, cover with foil, and continue roasting until tender.

SHISH KEBAB

To make 8 skewers

½ cup red wine
¼ cup olive oil
1 small onion, chopped
½ teaspoon salt
¼ teaspoon black pepper
⅛ teaspoon powdered sage
⅛ teaspoon dry mustard
⅛ teaspoon oregano
1½ pounds lamb cubes
16 medium-sized mushrooms
2 green peppers, cubed

Place a plastic bag in a deep bowl and fill with red wine, olive oil, chopped onion, salt, pepper, sage, mustard, and oregano. Mix well. Add lamb cubes and fasten bag with a wire closure. Marinate in refrigerator for at least 6 hours or overnight. To broil, skewer a whole mushroom cap onto a metal skewer about 8 inches long, then a cube of lamb; next alternate cubes of green pepper and cubes of lamb, and place a mushroom at the end. Line up skewers on a broiling pan, brush with remaining marinade, and broil for 5 minutes. Turn, brush with marinade, and broil for an additional 5 minutes or until lamb cubes are browned. Serve at once.

❧ 11 ❧

Praiseworthy Poultry

Do you know what the biggest bargain in price and protein is today? Chicken! It is in abundant supply, available in many sizes and in a variety of packaging to suit your every need. Chicken has a mild flavor and lends itself to many different kinds of seasonings. It may be served in different ways several times a week without creating monotonous dining.

Most chickens can be roasted if they are young and plump. Don't be misled by the label identifying certain chickens as broilers and fryers. This refers to their age and size but these chickens can also be roasted and potted if they are meaty enough. It is advisable, however, to use heavier fowl for soup and stewing, since they are meatier and have more flavor.

Raw poultry may be kept in the refrigerator for one or two days, if all the plastic wrappings have been removed and the poultry is rewrapped loosely in waxed paper. There should be some circulation of air around the chicken. Cooked chicken may be stored in the refrigerator for one or two days, but make sure to bring the gravy to the boiling point before re-serving it.

The leftover stuffing in chicken, turkey, or duck should be removed from the bird and stored in a separate, covered dish. The cold of the refrigerator will not penetrate to the core of the stuffing if it is left in the bird. You are therefore courting bacteria growth if you have stuffing in the bird.

Do be conscientious about the way you handle all foods to protect yourself from unnecessary illness. Develop the habit of storing in your refrigerator everything that is perishable. Too many otherwise sensible homemakers prepare food hours before it is needed, allow it to stay in the kitchen in a lukewarm state— an open invitation to bacteria—and then warm the food at a temperature too low to kill the bacteria. Result: a "virus" hits the family. There probably would be fewer cases of stomach virus if more care were exercised in the kitchen. If you want to do some stages of your cooking early in the day, by all means go ahead, but cool the food and put it into the refrigerator until you are ready to proceed with the rest of the cooking. Then heat the food at a reliable temperature: a boiling point for soups and gravies before you reduce heat to simmering, or an oven temperature of 325 degrees. It takes more than an apple a day to keep the doctor away.

ROASTING GUIDE FOR POULTRY

KIND	POUNDS	TOTAL ROASTING TIME HOURS AT 325 DEGREES F.
Chickens, whole	1½ to 2½	1 to 2
	2½ to 4½	2 to 3½
Capons, whole	5 to 8	2½ to 3½
Ducks, whole	4 to 6	2 to 3
Geese, whole	6 to 8	3 to 3½
	8 to 12	3½ to 4½
Turkeys, whole	6 to 8	3 to 3½
	8 to 12	3½ to 4½
	12 to 16	4½ to 5½
	16 to 20	5½ to 6½
	20 to 24	6½ to 7

CHICKEN IN THE POT

To serve 2 or 3	To serve 4 to 6
1 whole chicken (about 3 pounds)	2 whole chickens (about 3 pounds each)
1 cup whole canned tomatoes	2 cups whole canned tomatoes
1 cup chicken broth (may be canned)	2 cups chicken broth (may be canned)
1 onion, sliced	2 onions, sliced
1 green pepper, diced	2 green peppers, diced
½ pound fresh mushrooms	1 pound fresh mushrooms
½ teaspoon salt	1 teaspoon salt
¼ teaspoon pepper	½ teaspoon pepper
¼ teaspoon paprika	½ teaspoon paprika
½ teaspoon sugar	1 teaspoon sugar
½ cup white wine (optional)	1 cup white wine (optional)
2 tablespoons fresh dill, or 1 teaspoon dried dill	4 tablespoons fresh dill, or 2 teaspoons dried dill

Place chicken in a Dutch oven, or similar covered pot. Add tomatoes and broth. Arrange onion, green pepper, and mushrooms around the chicken. Sprinkle salt, pepper, paprika, and sugar over all. Pour wine over all. Sprinkle dill around the chicken. Cover the pot. Simmer on low heat for 1 hour, or until chicken can be pierced easily with a fork. Overcooked chicken will fall away from the bones. Spoon gravy over the chicken occasionally during the cooking to keep it moist. This recipe can be prepared in advance and reheated just before serving.

CHICKEN CACCIATORA

To serve 2 or 3	To serve 4 to 6
¼ cup olive oil	½ cup olive oil
¼ cup flour	½ cup flour
¼ teaspoon salt	½ teaspoon salt
⅛ teaspoon pepper	¼ teaspoon pepper
1 chicken, cut in parts	2 chickens, cut in parts
¼ pound ham, sliced thin	½ pound ham, sliced thin
1 onion, sliced	2 onions, sliced

½ green pepper, chopped fine   1 green pepper, chopped fine
1 clove garlic, peeled   1 or 2 cloves garlic, peeled
1 cup chicken broth   2 cups chicken broth
1 cup whole canned tomatoes   2 cups whole canned tomatoes
½ pound fresh mushrooms,   1 pound fresh mushrooms,
  sliced   sliced
½ teaspoon oregano   1 teaspoon oregano
¼ teaspoon salt   ½ teaspoon salt
½ teaspoon sugar   1 teaspoon sugar

Heat oil in a Dutch oven or similar covered pot. Combine flour, salt, and pepper in a small bag; shake chicken parts in bag to coat evenly. Brown chicken in the oil. Turn heat very low. Add ham, shredding it into small pieces. Add onion, green pepper, and garlic. Stir for several minutes. Add chicken broth, tomatoes, and sliced mushrooms. Sprinkle oregano, salt, and sugar over all; stir and cover. Simmer for 1 hour over low heat, or until chicken is easily pierced with a fork. This recipe can be prepared in advance and reheated just before serving.

CHICKEN BREASTS IN WHITE WINE SAUCE

To serve 2 or 3   *To serve 4 to 6*
4 halves chicken breasts   8 halves chicken breasts
1 tablespoon butter   2 tablespoons butter
½ onion, minced   1 onion, minced
1 tablespoon flour   2 tablespoons flour
½ cup broth (may be canned)   1 cup broth (may be canned)
½ cup white wine   1 cup white wine
1 teaspoon lemon juice   2 teaspoons lemon juice
½ teaspoon sugar   1 teaspoon sugar
¼ teaspoon salt   ½ teaspoon salt
⅛ teaspoon pepper   ¼ teaspoon pepper
¼ pound fresh mushrooms,   ½ pound fresh mushrooms,
  sliced   sliced

With a small sharp knife remove bones from breasts by running the blade along the bone structure. Arrange breasts in a flat casserole dish or roasting pan, in a single layer. In a small saucepan, melt butter. Add minced onion and stir over low heat for several minutes. Add flour and stir until mixture bubbles. Add broth and wine, stirring until smooth. Add lemon juice, sugar, salt, pepper, and sliced mushrooms. Simmer and stir until mixture thickens, about 3 minutes. Pour sauce over chicken breasts. Bake in a 350-degree oven for 25 minutes, occasionally basting with the sauce. This recipe can be prepared in advance, refrigerated, and then baked just before serving.

CHICKEN LIVER LUAU

To serve 2 or 3	*To serve 4 to 6*
⅛ *pound butter*	¼ *pound butter*
1 *onion, diced*	2 *onions, diced*
1 *green pepper, diced*	2 *green peppers, diced*
¼ *pound fresh mushrooms, sliced*	½ *pound fresh mushrooms, sliced*
1 *pound fresh chicken livers*	2 *pounds fresh chicken livers*
1 *(8-ounce) can pineapple chunks*	1 *(16-ounce) can pineapple chunks*
1 *tablespoon brown sugar*	2 *tablespoons brown sugar*
2 *teaspoons cornstarch*	1 *tablespoon cornstarch*
1 *teaspoon soy sauce*	2 *teaspoons soy sauce*

Melt butter in a large skillet. Add onion and green pepper; sauté until onions are translucent. Add sliced mushrooms; sauté for 3 minutes. Add livers; sauté until brown on 1 side, then turn over and add drained pineapple chunks, reserving pineapple liquid. Into the pineapple liquid, stir brown sugar, cornstarch, and soy sauce until dry ingredients are completely dissolved. Pour this mixture into the skillet and stir to coat livers thoroughly. Simmer for 3 to 5 minutes, stirring constantly to prevent sticking. Serve at once on a bed of rice.

CHICKEN IN PINEAPPLE SAUCE

To serve 2 or 3	*To serve 4 to 6*
6 *chicken thighs*	12 *chicken thighs*
2 *tablespoons flour*	¼ *cup flour*
⅛ *teaspoon nutmeg*	¼ *teaspoon nutmeg*
2 *tablespoons butter*	¼ *cup butter*

1 *(13-ounce) can pineapple*
   tidbits
1 *tablespoon cornstarch*
1 *tablespoon brown sugar*
¼ *teaspoon salt*
2 *tablespoons soy sauce*

2 *(13-ounce) cans pineapple*
   tidbits
2 *tablespoons cornstarch*
2 *tablespoons brown sugar*
½ *teaspoon salt*
¼ *cup soy sauce*

Dust chicken thighs (or other parts if you prefer) with flour and nutmeg. Melt butter in a skillet; brown chicken parts on all sides. In a separate small saucepan, combine the juice from the pineapple, cornstarch, brown sugar, salt, and soy sauce. Heat this sauce, stirring constantly until it boils and thickens. Remove from heat; add pineapple tidbits. Spoon over chicken parts in skillet; cover and simmer for 15 to 20 minutes. This recipe can be prepared in advance, refrigerated after adding sauce, and baked at 350 degrees for 20 minutes just before serving.

FRIED CHICKEN

To serve 2 or 3
¼ *cup fine bread crumbs*
½ *cup flour*
2 *teaspoons salt*
2 *teaspoons paprika*
¼ *teaspoon pepper*
¼ *teaspoon garlic powder*
1 *frying chicken, cut in parts*
½ *cup oil*

To serve 4 to 6
½ *cup fine bread crumbs*
1 *cup flour*
1 *heaping tablespoon salt*
1 *heaping tablespoon paprika*
½ *teaspoon pepper*
½ *teaspoon garlic powder*
2 *frying chickens, cut in parts*
1 *cup oil*

In a plastic bag, combine bread crumbs, flour, salt, paprika, pepper, and garlic powder. Mix thoroughly. Shake chicken parts in this bag, 2 or 3 pieces at a time, coating each piece well. Place coated chicken aside on a rack to let coating adhere. Meanwhile, heat oil in a large skillet; when bubbly, add coated chicken and brown on each side. Do a few pieces at a time, being careful not to crowd them. Remove chicken as it is browned. When all pieces are browned, return them to the skillet, cover, and simmer for about 25 minutes. Remove cover and crisp chicken by cooking over low heat another 10 minutes. Serve at once. Larger amounts may be browned and then placed in a roasting pan and baked in a 350-degree oven for 40 minutes.

ROAST DUCKLING WITH ORANGE–BRANDY SAUCE

To serve 4

1 *duckling (about 5 pounds)*

3 *oranges*

⅓ *cup cider vinegar*

2 *tablespoons sugar*

1 *lemon*

¼ *cup consomme (may be made with a bouillon cube)*

2 *tablespoons brandy*

Wash duck thoroughly; cut 1 orange in half and place both halves in the cavity of duck. Place duck in a roasting pan, and put in a 325-degree oven, uncovered, for about 1½ hours. Meanwhile, pare the rind from the 2 remaining oranges. Squeeze juice and set aside. Slice rind into long slivers and place in a saucepan; add just enough water to cover, and boil for about 2 minutes. Drain. Place vinegar and sugar in the saucepan. Simmer until sugar is dissolved; add the juice obtained from the 2 oranges. Squeeze lemon for juice, and add juice to the saucepan. Add drained orange rind. Simmer for 10 minutes, stirring occasionally. When duck is roasted, remove orange and place duck on a platter; add consomme and brandy to the pan juices (if there is a great deal of fat, remove it first). Add caramelized orange mixture and simmer, constantly stirring, for about 4 minutes. Spoon sauce over duck and serve at once.

ROAST TURKEY

To serve 6 to 8

1 *(12-pound) turkey*

1 *clove garlic, peeled*

1 *tablespoon salt*

1 *tablespoon paprika*

¼ *cup melted butter*

Clean, rinse, and drain turkey. Rub inside and out with the clove of garlic. Rub inside and out with salt. Place in large roasting pan. Stir paprika into melted butter and brush entire skin with the mixture, reserving some for basting during roasting. Cover top of turkey loosely with a large piece of aluminum foil, to be removed during the last hour of browning. Place in a 325-degree oven. Roast for about 4 hours, or until turkey leg moves easily and is tender when pierced with a long-tined fork. Baste with the butter–paprika mixture several times during the roasting.

QUICK-TRICK STUFFING:

1 *package prepared stuffing mix*
1 *large onion, sliced thin*
½ *pound mushrooms, sliced*
½ *cup butter*

Prepare stuffing as directed on the package. Sauté onion and mushrooms in butter; add to stuffing mixture. Fill cavity of turkey loosely with stuffing, tie legs to body, and roast as directed above. If there is turkey left over, remove stuffing before refrigerating.

CHERRY-GLAZED TURKEY ROLL

A QUICK-TRICK WAY

To serve 6 to 8
1 *(4- to 6-pound) frozen turkey roll*
½ *cup melted butter*
1 *teaspoon salt*
1 *can cherry pie filling*
½ *cup Burgundy wine*
1 *teaspoon allspice*
½ *teaspoon nutmeg*

Prepare and bake turkey roll according to the package instructions, basting frequently with the melted butter and salt mixture for last 15 minutes of baking time. Combine cherry pie filling, wine, allspice, and nutmeg. Spoon this glacé mixture over the turkey roll and return to the oven for an additional 15 minutes. Spoon over turkey slices as you serve.

❧ 12 ❧

Vegetables with Vigor

IF MOST VEGETABLES HAD ANY SPUNK THEY WOULD REBEL AGAINST the poor treatment they receive from refrigerator to table. Overcooked, underseasoned, and drably offered, it's no wonder they have become a sorry excuse for the colorful nutrient they should be. Well prepared, they could become your best source of nutrients and vitamins and supply endless variety to your menu.

Will Rogers said that he never met a man he didn't like. I will say that I've never seen a vegetable that could not be prepared in some form that you would like. Some years ago I faced the challenge of my brother who would not eat cauliflower. I served him a heaping portion of it French fried accompanied by an interesting sauce for dipping. He complimented me on the unusual fish course! He wouldn't believe that not only had he eaten the cauliflower he so disliked but he had raved about it to boot. Therefore, do not take your groom too seriously if he claims never to eat a certain vegetable. Do a little investigating to find out why that vegetable does not appeal to him, and then find a way to prepare it so that it will.

Why bother? Because vegetables are among the truly delicious foods. They provide color, texture, and taste diversion to a menu and can become the highlight of an otherwise simple meal. They are a veritable treasure trove for inventive cooks who are willing to learn how to protect the freshness and durability of each kind of vegetable.

Fresh, frozen, or canned vegetables offer a ready source of vitamins A and C along with minerals such as calcium and iron. To get the most food return for your fresh-food dollar, you must develop a knowing eye at the buying point. Here are some hints that will help you to select the best value for your money.

ASPARAGUS	Stalks should be mostly green (for more tenderness) with compact tips. Before refrigerating, remove tough white parts of stalks. Store in a plastic bag, preferably in the refrigerator crisper. Use within 1 or 2 days.
BEANS, lima	Choose well-filled pods that are clean, fresh, and of good color. If the pods are shriveled, spotted, or flabby, it is an indication of age and the beans will be tough and have poor flavor. Shelled lima beans should be plump, and of good green or green-white color. Refrigerate and use within 1 or 2 days.
BEANS, snap	Choose pods with small seeds, as overmature pods may become tough. Avoid dry-looking or wilted pods; the best taste is found in the freshest beans. Refrigerate and use within 1 or 2 days.
BEETS	Choose relatively smooth and firm beets. Soft or shriveled beets may be tough. If the beet tops are crisp and of dark green color, they may be used as a separate vegetable. Handle these greens as you would spinach leaves. Store beets, covered, in the refrigerator and use within 1 or 2 weeks.
BROCCOLI	Avoid broccoli with yellow flower clusters. Choose broccoli that is clean, with compact clusters. The stalks should be tender and firm, dark green in color. Dirty spots may indicate insects. Soak flower clusters thoroughly before using. Store in refrigerator in a plastic bag and use within 1 or 2 days.

BRUSSELS SPROUTS	Avoid sprouts with worm-eaten leaves, a dirty appearance, and wilted or yellowing leaves. Choose firm sprouts of good green color. Store in refrigerator in plastic bag. Use within 1 or 2 days.
CABBAGE	Choose crisp and firm heads that feel heavy for their size. Avoid cabbage with wormholes, discoloration, or softness. Store in plastic bag in refrigerator and use within 1 or 2 weeks.
CARROTS	Should be smooth and firm, with good color. Very large size may mean a pithy core. Avoid wilted or shriveled carrots, or those which are excessively cracked. Remove tips and tops and store in a plastic bag in refrigerator. Use within 1 or 2 weeks.
CAULIFLOWER	Choose white or creamy white, clean, firm, and compact head, with fresh green leaves. Avoid spotted or bruised heads. Soak well before using to insure absence of tiny insects. Store covered in refrigerator and use within 3 to 5 days.
CELERY	Choose crisp, clean celery of medium length, with branches that will snap easily. Avoid soft, pithy, or stringy celery. Wrap in plastic bag and store in crisper of refrigerator. Use within 1 to 2 weeks.
CORN	The best corn is the freshest picked. The best-quality corn is filled with plump kernels that are firm when pressed. Husks should also be fresh and green. If the husks look dry or yellowed, or the kernels are shriveled, don't purchase. Undeveloped kernels lack flavor when cooked; overdeveloped kernels will taste mealy. Cook as soon as possible after purchase.
CUCUMBERS	Choose firm, green-colored, well-shaped cucumbers. Avoid withered or shriveled cucum-

bers which may taste tough and bitter. Overmature cucumbers appear dull or yellowed in color and look puffy. Be sure the surface is firm without decay spots. Store in crisper of refrigerator. Use within 3 to 5 days

EGGPLANT   Choose a firm, uniformly dark rich purple heavy eggplant. Avoid scarred, wilted, or soft eggplant as the flavor may be poor or bitter. Decay appears as brown spots on the surface. Refrigerate in a plastic bag, or store in a cool place (about 60 degrees F.). Use within 1 or 2 days.

LETTUCE   Choose crisp, clean heads that are fairly firm. Avoid wilted heads, those that have an excess of outer leaves, and those that have rusty spots. Wash and dry thoroughly before storing. Wrap in paper toweling and store in the crisper of the refrigerator. Use within 1 or 2 days.

MUSHROOMS   Choose clean, white, firm mushrooms with light-colored gills on the underside. Brown or black gills indicate older mushrooms. Avoid discolored, wilted, or soft mushrooms. Store in plastic bags in the refrigerator and use within 1 or 2 days.

ONIONS   Choose clean, hard, well-shaped onions with dry skins. Avoid onions with developing seed-stem and those that feel moist at the neck, which is an indication of decay within. Store in a cool place at 60 degrees F. Onions will sprout or decay if the temperature or humidity is high, but they will keep for a month or so if the temperature is cool and dry.

PARSLEY   Choose leaves with a crisp appearance that are bright green and free of yellowed leaves. Avoid wilted, poorly colored parsley. Wash thoroughly. Dry and place in a tightly covered jar in the refrigerator. Use within 1 or 2 weeks.

99

PEAS	Choose fresh, well-filled pods that are uniformly light green in color and firm to the touch. Avoid flat immature peas, or wilted or yellowing peas. Leave in pods and store covered in the refrigerator. Use within 1 or 2 days. There is a distinct loss of sweetness if they are kept longer.
PEPPERS, bell	Choose firm, fresh-colored peppers. Avoid shriveled, dull-appearing, or spotted ones. Wash and dry. Store in the crisper or in plastic bags in the refrigerator and use within 3 to 5 days.
POTATOES	Choose firm, smooth, and well-shaped potatoes in a size corresponding to your use for them. Avoid sprouting, wilted, leathery, or discolored potatoes, and those developing a surface green color (they may be bitter). Store in a dark, dry place with good ventilation and a temperature of 45 to 50 degrees F. They may be kept for several months this way. If necessary, keep at room temperature and use within 1 week.
RADISHES	Choose smooth, firm, crisp radishes. Avoid wilted, decayed, and pithy ones. Remove tops and store in a plastic bag in the crisper of the refrigerator. Use within 1 or 2 weeks.
SPINACH	Leaves should be clean, fresh green in color, and crisp. Avoid wilted, bruised, and yellowed leaves. Decay appears as a slimy spot. Wash thoroughly and dry. Wrap in paper toweling and store in crisper of refrigerator until used. Use within 1 or 2 days.
TOMATOES	Choose well-formed, plump, uniformly red-colored tomatoes. Avoid those with bruise marks, and those that are overripe, or soft. Decay is usually indicated by mold growth or soft discolored areas. Store ripe tomatoes uncovered in the refrigerator crisper. Keep

unripe tomatoes at room temperature away from direct sunlight until ripe; then refrigerate. Use within 3 to 5 days.

ZUCCHINI   Choose small crisp zucchini of dark green color. Avoid soft spots. Look for signs of mold growth and wilted appearance. Wash, dry, and wrap in plastic. Store in refrigerator. Use within 3 to 5 days.

When selecting canned vegetables, purchase the best quality that you can afford. Once you have found a good brand, stick with it for reliable purchasing. Store cans at room temperature, and rotate them in order of purchase. Avoid cans with bulging tops or those that are dented and rusted.

When choosing frozen vegetables, buy packages that feel solid to the touch. Avoid packages that are stored above the safety line in your grocer's freezer; dig down deep for the firmest packages. Have your frozen foods packed together in one bag for easier and faster handling from grocer to your freezer. This should be the first bag that you unpack.

In order to lose the least amount of vitamins during cooking, you will have to take some precautionary measures. Wash all vegetables thoroughly, even if they look clean. Cook them in the least amount of water or liquid possible, for the least amount of time possible. If the vegetable is one that needs scraping or peeling, be sure to remove as little of the outer covering as possible to avoid losing the valuable minerals right beneath the skin. Avoid heating and reheating vegetables; the loss in flavor and vitamins will make the serving almost worthless.

Baking is the best method for retaining the most vitamins; waterless cooking comes next. Steaming is also an excellent method; boiling is the least desirable. Since most cooks choose to boil their vegetables, special care must be taken to retain both vitamins and color. If overcooked, green vegetables tend to turn a brownish color; cook them in an uncovered pot with perhaps the tiniest pinhead dot of baking soda if you want to retain the bright green color. Lemon juice will keep white vegetables from becoming an unappealing beige, and it will keep red vegetables like red cabbage and beets from turning brown. Yellow vegetables, which should be cooked, covered, in a minimum of water, need no additives to retain their color.

The recipes in this chapter were chosen for their originality, taste appeal, and male approval. They include many quick-trick ways to turn the ordinary vegetable into a second-helping success.

GREEN BEANS AMANDINE

A QUICK-TRICK WAY

To serve 2 or 3

1 *(16-ounce) can French-style green beans*

1 *tablespoon butter*

1 *tablespoon slivered almonds*

To serve 4 to 6

2 *(16-ounce) cans French-style green beans*

2 *tablespoons butter*

2 *tablespoons slivered almonds*

Heat green beans in a saucepan. Drain. Add butter and stir until melted. Serve topped with slivered almonds.

GREEN BEANS GOURMET

A QUICK-TRICK WAY

To serve 2 or 3

½ *(1-pound) can cooked wild rice*

1 *(10-ounce) package green beans (diagonal-cut and frozen in mushroom sauce in cooking pouch)*

½ *cup grated American cheese*

1 *tablespoon toasted sesame seeds*

To serve 4 to 6

1 *(1-opund) can cooked wild rice*

2 *(10-ounce) packages green beans (diagonal-cut and frozen in mushroom sauce in cooking pouch)*

1 *cup grated American cheese*

2 *tablespoons toasted sesame seeds*

Empty wild rice into top of a double boiler and heat through. Cook green beans as directed on package. Combine beans with rice in a 1-quart casserole; top with American cheese and sesame seeds. Slip under the broiler for 2 to 3 minutes, until cheese is lightly browned. Serve at once.

LEMON-BUTTERED CABBAGE

To serve 2 or 3
2 tablespoons butter
½ large head cabbage,
    shredded
¼ teaspoon grated lemon peel
1 tablespoon lemon juice
¼ teaspoon celery seed
¼ teaspoon salt
Dash of pepper

To serve 4 to 6
¼ cup butter
1 large head cabbage,
    shredded
½ teaspoon grated lemon peel
2 tablespoons lemon juice
½ teaspoon celery seed
½ teaspoon salt
⅛ teaspoon pepper

Melt butter in a large skillet. Add shredded cabbage. Cover and cook, stirring occasionally, about 6 to 8 minutes, or until just tender. Add lemon peel, lemon juice, celery seed, salt, and pepper. Serve at once.

CARROTS VERONIQUE

A QUICK-TRICK WAY

To serve 2 or 3
1 (10-ounce) package frozen
    carrots in butter sauce,
    in boilable pouch
⅛ teaspoon sugar
½ cup seedless grapes
1 tablespoon white wine

To serve 4 to 6
2 (10-ounce) packages frozen
    carrots in butter sauce,
    in boilable pouch
¼ teaspoon sugar
1 cup seedless grapes
2 tablespoons white wine

Heat carrots as directed on package. Empty carrots and butter sauce into a small skillet. Add sugar, grapes, and wine. Cover and simmer for 3 minutes. Serve at once.

ELEGANT CARROTS

A QUICK-TRICK WAY

To serve 2 or 3
1 (1-pound) can sliced carrots
1 bouillon cube
2 tablespoons butter
1 tablespoon brown sugar
1 teaspoon chopped parsley

To serve 4 to 6
2 (1-pound) cans sliced carrots
2 bouillon cubes
¼ cup butter
2 tablespoons brown sugar
2 teaspoons chopped parsley

Drain juice from carrots into a saucepan; add bouillon cube and heat juice until cube is dissolved. Add butter and sugar, stirring until dissolved. Add sliced carrots; simmer until most of liquid is evaporated. Serve with a sprinkling of chopped parsley.

FRENCH FRIED CAULIFLOWER

To serve 2 or 3	*To serve 4 to 6*
1 *egg, slightly beaten*	2 *eggs, slightly beaten*
⅓ *cup milk*	⅔ *cup milk*
1 *tablespoon melted butter*	2 *tablespoons melted butter*
½ *cup sifted flour*	1 *cup sifted flour*
½ *teaspoon baking powder*	1 *teaspoon baking powder*
1 *teaspoon sugar*	2 *teaspoons sugar*
½ *teaspoon salt*	1 *teaspoon salt*
1 *small head cauliflower*	1 *large or 2 small heads cauliflower*
½ *cup cooking oil*	1 *cup cooking oil*

Combine egg, milk, and melted butter. Stir in flour, baking powder, sugar, and salt. Wash cauliflower thoroughly and cut into large flowerets. Heat oil in a skillet. Dip flowerets into batter and fry in hot fat until well browned. Drain on paper towels. This recipe can be fried and drained, then reheated in a 350-degree oven until hot and crisp.

MUSHROOM SAUCE ON RICE RING

A QUICK-TRICK WAY

To serve 4 to 6

1 *(6-ounce) package whole mushrooms frozen in butter sauce*

1 *green pepper, chopped*

1 *(28-ounce) can tomatoes*

1 *(8-ounce) can tomato paste*

½ *clove garlic, minced*

1 *teaspoon sugar*

¼ *teaspoon oregano*

¼ *teaspoon salt*

⅛ *teaspoon pepper*
4 *cups hot cooked rice, instant cooking variety*
2 *tablespoons butter*

Remove frozen mushrooms from pouch and sauté for 5 minutes in a skillet. Add green pepper and stir. Add tomatoes, tomato paste, garlic, sugar, oregano, salt, and pepper. Simmer for 20 minutes. Meanwhile, add butter to hot rice, tossing lightly. Fill a 1-quart ring mold with rice mixture; set in a pan of hot water until ready to serve. Unmold rice on a warm platter just before serving. Fill center of rice ring with mushroom sauce.

FRENCH FRIED ONION RINGS

A QUICK-TRICK WAY

To serve 2 or 3
2 *large Bermuda onions*
1 *cup prepared pancake batter*
½ *teaspoon salt*
1 *cup cooking oil*

To serve 4 to 6
4 *large Bermuda onions*
2 *cups prepared pancake batter*
1 *teaspoon salt*
2 *cups cooking oil*

Peel and slice onions into ¼-inch-thick slices. Prepare pancake batter according to directions on package; add salt. Heat oil in a skillet; when bubbling, dip onions into batter, then fry until golden brown. Remove each batch onto paper toweling to drain. Serve hot and crisp.

BAKED STUFFED POTATOES

To serve 2
2 *baking potatoes*
¼ *teaspoon salt*
1 *tablespoon butter*
2 *tablespoons dairy sour cream*
1 *tablespoon grated cheddar cheese*
Paprika

Bake potatoes in a 350-degree oven or top-of-stove potato baker until soft and mealy. Remove from oven and slice tops off lengthwise. Scoop potatoes into a bowl, taking care to leave the bottom halves of skin intact. Reserve bottom skins. To potatoes, add salt, butter, sour cream, and cheddar cheese. Whip well until potato mixture is fluffy. Add some milk if the mixture seems dry. Fill reserved potato bottoms with whipped potato mixture and dash paprika over the top. They may be refrigerated or frozen at this point. Just before serving, heat in a 350-degree oven until tops form a slightly browned crust. Serve at once.

PARSLEYED POTATOES

To serve 2 or 3	*To serve 4 to 6*
¾ *pound tiny new potatoes*	1½ *pounds tiny new potatoes*
2 *tablespoons butter*	¼ *cup butter*
2 *tablespoons minced parsley*	¼ *cup minced parsley*
1 *teaspoon lemon juice*	2 *teaspoons lemon juice*

Wash potatoes, leaving them whole with skins intact. Place them in a saucepan, cover with salted water, and boil for about 15 minutes, or until potatoes are tender. In a small saucepan, melt butter; remove from heat and stir in parsley and lemon juice. Pour into a small deep serving dish. Peel potatoes quickly and place in lemon–butter sauce. Roll potatoes in sauce with a spoon until well coated. Serve at once.

SCALLOPED POTATOES

To serve 2 or 3	*To serve 4 to 6*
1 *tablespoon flour*	2 *tablespoons flour*
½ *teaspoon salt*	1 *teaspoon salt*
Dash of pepper	⅛ *teaspoon pepper*
2 *cups thinly sliced potatoes*	4 *cups thinly sliced potatoes*
1 *small onion, diced*	1 *large onion, diced*
1 *tablespoon butter*	2 *tablespoons butter*
¾ *cup milk, scalded*	1½ *cups milk, scalded*
¼ *teaspoon paprika*	¼ *teaspoon paprika*

Combine flour, salt, and pepper. Arrange a layer of potatoes in a greased casserole. Top with some of the diced onion, then a layer of the flour mixture. Dot with butter. Repeat layers, ending with a layer of potatoes. Pour scalded milk over all. Sprinkle with paprika. Cover and bake in a 375-degree oven for about 45 minutes; uncover and bake 15 minutes longer, or until potatoes are tender.

POTATO SALAD

To serve 2 or 3

1½ cups sliced potatoes, boiled
1 small onion, chopped
½ teaspoon sugar
½ teaspoon vinegar
½ teaspoon salt
½ teaspoon celery seed
1 hard-cooked egg, diced
½ cup mayonnaise
¼ cup dairy sour cream

To serve 4 to 6

3 cups sliced potatoes, boiled
1 large onion, chopped
1 teaspoon sugar
1 teaspoon vinegar
1 teaspoon salt
1 teaspoon celery seed
2 hard-cooked eggs, diced
1 cup mayonnaise
½ cup dairy sour cream

Place sliced boiled potatoes and chopped onion in a bowl. Sprinkle with sugar, vinegar, salt, and celery seed, and stir through. Add diced egg. Combine mayonnaise and sour cream Add to potatoes, and fold through to coat them thoroughly. Refrigerate until ready to serve. Sprinkle with a dusting of paprika and garnish with parsley.

SWEET POTATO CASSEROLE

A QUICK-TRICK WAY

To serve 4 to 6

1 (23-ounce) can whole sweet potatoes, drained
1 (1-pound) can whole baby carrots, drained
1 (20-ounce) jar applesauce with apricot chunks
2 tablespoons butter
2 tablespoons brown sugar

Combine drained sweet potatoes and carrots in a 1-quart buttered casserole. Add applesauce with apricot chunks and mix through. Dot the top with butter and sprinkle brown sugar over all. Bake in a 350-degree oven for 25 minutes. Serve hot.

PRALINE YAMS

To serve 2 or 3	To serve 4 to 6
1 *(16-ounce) can yams,* *drained*	2 *(16-ounce) cans yams,* *drained*
1 *tablespoon butter*	2 *tablespoons butter*
¼ *cup heavy cream*	½ *cup heavy cream*
¼ *cup brown sugar*	½ *cup brown sugar*
¼ *cup chopped pecans*	½ *cup chopped pecans*
⅛ *teaspoon salt*	¼ *teaspoon salt*
⅛ *teaspoon cinnamon*	¼ *teaspoon cinnamon*
⅛ *teaspoon nutmeg*	¼ *teaspoon nutmeg*

Arrange yams in a baking dish. In a small saucepan, over low heat, melt butter. Add cream, sugar, pecans, salt, cinnamon, and nutmeg; simmer and stir for about 5 minutes. Pour mixture over yams. Bake for 20 minutes in a 350-degree oven. This recipe can be prepared in advance, refrigerated, then baked just before serving.

CREAMED SPINACH

A QUICK-TRICK WAY

To serve 2 or 3	To serve 4 to 6
1 *(10-ounce) package frozen* *chopped spinach*	2 *(10-ounce) packages frozen* *chopped spinach*
½ *onion, grated*	1 *onion, grated*
⅛ *teaspoon nutmeg*	¼ *teaspoon nutmeg*
½ *(10½-ounce) can condensed* *cream of mushroom soup*	1 *(10½-ounce) can condensed* *cream of mushroom soup*

Empty frozen chopped spinach into a saucepan with amount of water as directed on package. Add onion and nutmeg. Cook as directed. Drain well. Stir in cream of mushroom soup and keep hot in the top of a double boiler until serving time.

SPICY STEWED TOMATOES

To serve 2 or 3

1 (1-pound) can whole
    tomatoes
½ teaspoon instant minced
    onion
¼ teaspoon ground oregano
⅛ teaspoon pepper
1 teaspoon sugar
⅓ cup fine bread crumbs
2 tablespoons butter

To serve 4 to 6

2 (1-pound) cans whole
    tomatoes
1 teaspoon instant minced
    onion
½ teaspoon ground oregano
¼ teaspoon pepper
2 teaspoons sugar
⅔ cup fine bread crumbs
¼ cup butter

Combine all ingredients in a saucepan. Simmer for 10 minutes, stirring occasionally. Serve at once.

ZUCCHINI

To serve 2 or 3

1 tablespoon butter
1 small onion, minced
2 zucchini
2 stalks celery, sliced thin
⅛ teaspoon salt
Dash of pepper
⅛ teaspoon thyme
¼ teaspoon paprika

To serve 4 to 6

2 tablespoons butter
1 large onion, minced
4 zucchini
4 stalks celery, sliced thin
¼ teaspoon salt
⅛ teaspoon pepper
¼ teaspoon thyme
½ teaspoon paprika

Melt butter in a large skillet. Add minced onion and sauté for several minutes until golden. Add zucchini sliced ½ inch thick. Add celery, salt, pepper, thyme, and paprika. Stir to distribute seasonings evenly. Cover and simmer for 10 minutes, or until zucchini is tender. Serve at once.

ZUCCHINI AND TOMATOES

To serve 2 or 3

1 *small onion, diced*
2 *tablespoons olive oil*
1 *(1-pound) can plum*
  tomatoes
½ *teaspoon salt*
¼ *teaspoon pepper*
½ *teaspoon oregano*
¼ *teaspoon thyme*
2 *teaspoons grated Parmesan*
  cheese
2 *zucchini, sliced ¼ inch thick*

To serve 4 to 6

1 *large onion, diced*
3 *tablespoons olive oil*
2 *(1-pound) cans plum*
  tomatoes
1 *teaspoon salt*
½ *teaspoon pepper*
1 *teaspoon oregano*
½ *teaspoon thyme*
1 *tablespoon grated Parmesan*
  cheese
4 *zucchini, sliced ¼ inch thick*

Sauté onion in olive oil in a large skillet. Add tomatoes, breaking up with the side of a kitchen spoon. Add salt, pepper, oregano, thyme, and Parmesan cheese. Simmer, covered, for 10 minutes. Add sliced zucchini, cover, and simmer for 10 to 15 minutes, or until zucchini is tender. Serve hot.

❧13❧

Pasta Know-how

To know your noodles these days takes a liberal education, but a walk down the pasta aisle of your supermarket will do for a start. Don't stop at spaghetti. Examine the packages of macaroni; the noodles in all widths, including those green with spinach; the wheels and shells and bows; the wide cannelloni noodles with tunnels for stuffing; the flat lasagne noodles with fluted edges; the soup noodles in strings, alphabets, and tiny squares—there are oodles of noodles to diversify your meal planning!

A universal food, pasta is thought to have originated in China though it gained its fame in Italy. The cuisine of most countries includes some form of pasta.

The most important thing to remember about cooking pasta is to use a large pot of salted boiling water, roughly four quarts of water for every pound of pasta. Add the pasta slowly so the water never stops boiling. One trick recommended by many cooks is to add a little cooking oil to the water to prevent the pasta from sticking together. Cook at a rapid boil following the cooking time prescribed on the package until the pasta is "al dente," tender but still chewy. Drain, and immediately proceed with the rest of your recipe.

A simple way to serve long strands of noodles is to add melted butter and a generous amount of grated Parmesan cheese. Another is to add white or red clam sauce. Perhaps the most popular way is to add a tomato sauce with or without meat.

Included in this chapter are some recipes to prepare at the last moment, and others which need to be prepared in advance though the final baking in a casserole may be done just before serving.

I have also included a recipe for a basic homemade cannelloni dish. It is not made like a noodle but from a batter—forming a thin crepe. The filling is folded into each crepe and then the crepes are lined up in a flat baking dish, covered with sauce, and placed in the oven for thirty minutes. A variety of fillings and a prize-winning white cheese sauce make this a company dish which may be served as a first course, a main course, or a side dish to a meat course, always to the accompaniment of raves. This dish does take a little time and effort, so try it on one of those days when you have a lot of time and feel creative. It is decidedly not a quick-trick dish, but it is one of my favorite inventions.

Take advantage of the variety that pasta can bring to your table, and think about different ways in which to add it in some form to your menu. It is wholesome, reasonably priced, and enjoyed by most people. Do explore its possibilities.

FETTUCINI ALFREDO

To serve 2 or 3
8 *ounces ¼-inch-wide noodles*
¼ *pound sweet butter, melted*
¼ *pound grated Parmesan cheese*
½ *cup heavy cream*

To serve 4 to 6
1 *pound ¼-inch-wide noodles*
½ *pound sweet butter, melted*
½ *pound grated Parmesan cheese*
1 *cup heavy cream*

Cook noodles according to the directions on package. Drain. Pour butter over noodles; alternately, stir in Parmesan cheese and cream. Toss noodles lightly. Serve hot at once.

NOODLE PUDDING WITH CHEESE AND RAISINS

To serve 6

1 *(8-ounce) package noodles, medium width*
3 *eggs*
½ *pound creamed cottage cheese*
½ *pint dairy sour cream*
¼ *teaspoon salt*
½ *cup sugar*
2 *tablespoons lemon juice*
½ *cup white seedless raisins*
⅓ *cup butter*
¼ *cup bread crumbs*

Preheat oven to 350 degrees. Cook noodles according to directions on package. Drain. Beat eggs; add cottage cheese and sour cream. Add salt, sugar, lemon juice, and raisins. Fold noodles into this mixture. Put half of the butter in a 7½-inch-by-12-inch baking dish, heat in the oven until butter is melted, then pour in noodle mixture. Dot top with remaining butter and bread crumbs. Bake for 1 hour. This pudding may be baked in greased muffin tins for approximately 30 minutes, and served in individual portions. The leftover noodle muffins may be frozen in a plastic bag and reheated in the muffin tin at a later date.

GREEN NOODLES IN SPINACH SAUCE

To serve 2 or 3	*To serve 4 to 6*
8 *ounces green noodles*	16 *ounces green noodles*
6 *spinach leaves*	12 *spinach leaves*
2 *sprigs parsley*	4 *sprigs parsley*
¼ *cup grated Parmesan cheese*	½ *cup grated Parmesan cheese*
1 *clove garlic, peeled*	2 *cloves garlic, peeled*
¼ *teaspoon salt*	½ *teaspoon salt*
¼ *cup broken walnuts*	½ *cup broken walnuts*
2 *tablespoons olive oil*	¼ *cup olive oil*
2 *tablespoons hot water*	¼ *cup hot water*

Cook green noodles as directed on package; drain. Place all other ingredients into a blender. Blend into a fine sauce. Pour over green noodles and serve at once.

SPAGHETTI WITH WHITE CLAM SAUCE

To serve 2 or 3	*To serve 4 to 6*
1 *can minced clams*	2 *cans minced clams*
¼ *cup olive oil*	½ *cup olive oil*
2 *cloves garlic, minced*	3 *cloves garlic, minced*
1 *tablespoon chopped parsley*	2 *tablespoons chopped parsley*
¼ *teaspoon salt*	½ *teaspoon salt*
⅛ *teaspoon pepper*	¼ *teaspoon pepper*
8 *ounces spaghetti*	1 *pound spaghetti*

Drain clams. Heat olive oil in a skillet. Add garlic and brown lightly. Add parsley, clams, salt, and pepper. Stir and simmer several minutes; remove from heat. Meanwhile, cook spaghetti according to directions on package. Drain. Pour onto a warm platter and pour clam sauce over. Toss lightly and serve hot.

SPAGHETTI MILANESE

To serve 2 or 3	*To serve 4 to 6*
2 *tablespoons olive oil*	¼ *cup olive oil*
1 *small onion, diced*	1 *large onion, diced*
½ *cup sliced mushrooms*	1 *cup sliced mushrooms*
1 *clove garlic, minced*	2 *cloves garlic, minced*
4 *chicken livers*	8 *chicken livers*
½ *teaspoon oregano*	1 *teaspoon oregano*
¼ *teaspoon salt*	½ *teaspoon salt*
⅛ *teaspoon pepper*	¼ *teaspoon pepper*
1 *(1-pound) can Italian toma-toes, packed in sauce with basil leaf*	2 *(1-pound) cans Italian toma-toes, packed in sauce with basil leaf*
8 *ounces spaghetti*	1 *pound spaghetti*

Heat oil in a skillet. Add diced onion, sliced mushrooms, and minced garlic; sauté until onions are golden. Cut chicken livers into small chunks; add to skillet and brown on all sides. Add oregano, salt, and pepper. Add tomatoes (if tomatoes are not packed with basil leaf, add ½ teaspoon basil); break tomatoes with the side of a spoon. Simmer for 15 minutes. Meanwhile, cook spaghetti as directed on package. Drain. Pour onto a warm platter. Pour sauce over and toss lightly to coat the pasta. Serve hot at once.

SPAGHETTI WITH TOMATO–MEAT SAUCE

To serve 2 or 3	*To serve 4 to 6*
2 *tablespoons olive oil*	3 *tablespoons olive oil*
1 *onion, diced*	1 *large onion, diced*
½ *green pepper, diced*	1 *green pepper, diced*
¼ *pound chopped beef*	½ *pound chopped beef*
1 *(1-pound) can Italian tomatoes*	2 *(1-pound) cans Italian tomatoes*
1 *(6-ounce) can tomato paste*	2 *(6-ounce) cans tomato paste*
½ *teaspoon salt*	1 *teaspoon salt*
⅛ *teaspoon pepper*	¼ *teaspoon pepper*
¼ *teaspoon oregano*	½ *teaspoon oregano*
8 *ounces spaghetti*	1 *pound spaghetti*

Heat oil in a large skillet. Sauté onion and green pepper. Add chopped beef and break into tiny bits with fork. Brown well. Stir in tomatoes and tomato paste. Add salt, pepper, and oregano. Simmer, covered, for 2 hours. Fifteen minutes before you are ready to serve, cook spaghetti according to directions on package. Drain. Place on a warm platter and pour tomato–meat sauce over pasta. Serve at once.

CRAB MEAT TETRAZZINI

A QUICK-TRICK WAY

To serve 2 or 3	To serve 4 to 6
2 tablespoons butter	3 tablespoons butter
1 small onion, diced fine	1 large onion, diced fine
½ green pepper, chopped	1 green pepper, chopped
1 (10½-ounce) can condensed cream of mushroom soup	2 (10½-ounce) cans condensed cream of mushroom soup
¼ cup milk	½ cup milk
2 tablespoons grated Parmesan cheese	¼ cup grated Parmesan cheese
1 tablespoon sherry	2 tablespoons sherry
8 ounces spaghetti	1 pound spaghetti
1 (6-ounce) can crab meat	2 (6-ounce) cans crab meat
Bread crumbs	Bread crumbs

Melt butter in a saucepan. Sauté diced onion and chopped green pepper until both are limp and onion is golden. Stir in mushroom soup, milk, and grated Parmesan cheese. Stir in sherry. Cover and simmer while spaghetti is cooking. Cook spaghetti according to directions on package. Drain. Pour into a well-greased casserole. Break crab meat into bite-sized pieces and add to spaghetti. Pour hot sauce over all and toss lightly. Top with a sprinkling of bread crumbs and bake for 30 minutes in a 350-degree oven. Serve at once.

BAKED MACARONI AND CHEESE

To serve 2 or 3	To serve 4 to 6
1 tablespoon butter	2 tablespoons butter
1 tablespoon flour	2 tablespoons flour
¼ teaspoon salt	½ teaspoon salt
⅛ teaspoon pepper	¼ teaspoon pepper
1 cup hot milk	2 cups hot milk
1 cup diced cheddar cheese	2 cups diced cheddar cheese
8 ounces macaroni	1 pound macaroni

In a saucepan, melt butter and stir in flour, salt, and pepper. Gradually stir in hot milk and cook, stirring until the sauce is thickened. Add cheddar cheese and stir until it is melted. Cook macaroni as directed on package. Drain. Lightly grease a casserole and pour hot sauce into it; stir in cooked macaroni. Bake for 20 minutes in a 350-degree oven. Serve hot.

BAKED MACARONI AND CHEESE

A QUICK-TRICK WAY

To serve 2 or 3

8 *ounces elbow macaroni*

½ *(10½-ounce) can condensed cream of mushroom soup*

2 *tablespoons grated Parmesan cheese*

2 *tablespoons bread crumbs*

1½ *teaspoons butter*

To serve 4 to 6

1 *pound elbow macaroni*

1 *(10½-ounce) can condensed cream of mushroom soup*

¼ *cup grated Parmesan cheese*

¼ *cup bread crumbs*

1 *tablespoon butter*

Cook elbow macaroni in boiling water, as directed on package. Drain. Empty into a greased casserole. Add cream of mushroom soup and grated Parmesan cheese; mix through thoroughly. Sprinkle top with bread crumbs and dot with butter. Bake in a 350-degree oven for 25 minutes.

MACARONI SALAD

To serve 4 or 6

8 *ounces elbow macaroni, cooked and drained*

1½ *cups diced celery*

1 *small onion, minced*

2 *pimientos, chopped*

1 *green pepper, chopped*

1 *teaspoon salt*

¼ *teaspoon pepper*

½ *cup mayonnaise*

½ *cup dairy sour cream*

2 *tablespoons lemon juice*

Drain cooked macaroni. Combine the rest of the ingredients in a deep bowl; stir well. Empty macaroni into the bowl and stir through. Refrigerate until serving time.

MUSHROOM CREPES

To make 12 crepes

CREPES:

2 *eggs*
⅔ *cup milk*
1 *tablespoon melted shortening*
½ *cup sifted flour*
¼ *teaspoon salt*

Beat eggs well; add milk and shortening. Sift flour and salt together and add to mixture. Beat with egg beater until smooth. Add more milk if necessary to make batter consistency of heavy cream. Brush small 5-inch skillet with shortening. Spoon 2 to 3 tablespoons of crepe batter into skillet, tipping pan to cover bottom evenly with batter. Cook, turning once, until light brown on both sides. Crepes can be prepared in advance and stored in refrigerator between layers of waxed paper.

FILLING:

3 *tablespoons butter*
1 *medium onion, chopped*
3 *cups sliced fresh mushrooms (about 18)*
¼ *cup lemon juice*
1 *(12-ounce) can or bottle beer*
3 *tablespoons heavy cream*
8 *ounces grated Gruyère cheese*
¼ *pound cooked ham, cut in thin strips*
½ *teaspoon cornstarch*
1 *teaspoon water*
⅛ *teaspoon salt*
Dash of pepper

In skillet, melt butter and sauté onion and mushrooms for 3 minutes. Sprinkle mushrooms generously with lemon juice to retain light color. Pour in beer and bring to a boil. Reduce heat and stir in cream. Simmer, stirring, until sauce is blended and slightly reduced, about 5 minutes. Add cheese, reserving half a cup for topping. Add ham and stir until cheese melts. Dissolve cornstarch in water and add to sauce, stirring until sauce thickens slightly. Add salt and pepper. Place 2 tablespoons of mixture in center of cooked crepe and roll. Arrange crepes in shallow oven-proof dish and sprinkle remaining cheese over top. Place under broiler for a minute until cheese is melted and lightly browned.

CANNELLONI AU GRATIN

To make 6 crepes	*To make 12 crepes*
CREPES:	**CREPES:**
1½ tablespoons melted butter	3 tablespoons melted butter
1 egg, beaten	2 eggs, beaten
⅛ teaspoon sugar	¼ teaspoon sugar
⅛ teaspoon salt	¼ teaspoon salt
3 tablespoons flour	⅓ cup flour
⅓ cup milk	⅔ cup milk

Add melted butter to beaten egg. Add sugar, salt, and flour. Mix until smooth. Add milk and stir. Lightly butter a 6-inch skillet and place over low heat. Spoon 2 to 3 tablespoons of the batter into the skillet and, working quickly, tilt the pan so that the entire bottom is covered with batter. When crepe is a solid circle and lightly browned on the bottom, tap it out upside down onto a clean dish towel. Re-butter the skillet to make each crepe until all the batter is used.

FILLING:	**FILLING:**
¼ cup cooked spinach, chopped	½ cup cooked spinach, chopped
1 cup cooked chicken, ground	2 cups cooked chicken, ground
2 tablespoons grated Parmesan cheese	¼ cup grated Parmesan cheese
⅓ cup chicken broth	⅔ cup chicken broth

Stir spinach, chicken, cheese, and broth together in a large skillet. Cover and simmer over low heat for 10 minutes, adding more broth if necessary to keep the mixture from sticking. Stir occasionally. To fill crepes, place about ¼ cup of the filling in the center of each crepe; push filling with a spoon until it forms a rectangle about 1½ inches by 3 inches on each crepe circle. Fold over 1 long side, then fold over the 2 short ends, then fold over the last long side, sealing the filling into a 3-inch-long roll. Place in a lightly greased flat casserole, side by side. Cover with sauce and bake.

SAUCE:	SAUCE:
3 *tablespoons butter*	6 *tablespoons butter*
3 *tablespoons flour*	6 *tablespoons flour*
1½ *cups milk*	3 *cups milk*
¼ *cup grated Parmesan cheese*	½ *cup grated Parmesan cheese*
¼ *teaspoon salt*	½ *teaspoon salt*
⅛ *teaspoon pepper*	¼ *teaspoon pepper*
⅛ *teaspoon nutmeg*	¼ *teaspoon nutmeg*

In a saucepan, melt butter. Stir in flour, and when the mixture is bubbling, stir in milk. Bring the sauce to a boil, stirring constantly. Remove from heat. Add cheese, salt, pepper, and nutmeg, stirring well. Spoon sauce over the filled crepes. Top with additional grated Parmesan cheese if desired. Bake for 30 minutes in a 350-degree oven. Serve 2 or more crepes per serving.

🍃 14 🍃

Shimmering Salads

SOMETIMES THE MOST EYE-APPEALING DISH AND THE ONE THAT wins the most praise is the easiest dish to make. Gelatin salad molds belong in this category. You will need several metal molds and at least one of them should be in ring form. You will also have to learn a few basic rules in order to avoid the disasters that sometimes occur.

One disaster is a gelatin mixture that does not come out of the mold in one piece. Another is a runny, capsizing offering which, upon being released from its girdling mold, sags all over the platter. Another is an incompletely dissolved gelatin that tastes gritty even though it looks pretty. The mishap that is probably the most unfortunate is a salad mold that wasn't worth your effort; the recipe is poor and the ingredients should never have been combined in something as binding as gelatin.

To guarantee success with gelatin molds, be certain to dissolve the gelatin completely in boiling liquid before adding cold liquid. For large molds, decrease the amount of liquid called for on the package by at least one-third cup to assure a firm consistency. The more rigid you want the mold to be, the less liquid you must use, keeping in mind that the normal ratio is one three-ounce package of gelatin to two cups of liquid.

Do not add fresh or frozen pineapple, figs, mangoes, or

papayas or frozen fruit juice blends containing these fruits. An enzyme in these fresh fruits prevents the gelatin from setting. However, when cooked or canned these fruits are fine to use.

To avoid the possibility of fruit and vegetables floating or sinking instead of being evenly suspended through the gelatin, chill the gelatin mixture until it has the consistency of egg white and then proceed to add the other ingredients.

If you take the precaution of brushing a light coating of salad oil over the entire interior surface of the mold, turning it upside down on absorbent paper to drain off the excess oil, you should have no trouble releasing the gelatin from the mold. Before unmolding gelatin, be sure that it is completely firm. Dip a small pointed knife in warm water and run the tip of it around the top edge of the mold to loosen the gelatin. Then quickly dip the mold in warm water for about ten seconds, making certain that the water does not flow over the rim into the gelatin. Place a chilled platter over the top and invert the mold.

If you still have difficulty unmolding gelatin, oil the mold and then place a long strip of aluminum foil, about one inch wide, across the bottom and up and over the sides, pressing it to conform to the shape of the mold. To remove gelatin, gently pull one of the tabs of aluminum foil to break the vacuum in the mold; then proceed as above to remove the mold and the foil strip.

If you wish to change the texture and appearance of the gelatin, chill it first until very thick and then beat with a rotary or electric mixer until the mixture is fluffy and thick. Next add the additional ingredients and return to the refrigerator until firm.

Layer effects can be created by mixing different colors of gelatin and chilling them firm, one layer at a time, until the entire mold is filled and chilled firm.

Be sure that your choice of a gelatin recipe complements the rest of your menu. I have included a number of recipes that will bring agreeable murmurs of pleasure every time you serve them. Each recipe has passed the male comment test: "I usually don't like these icky-sticky gelatin things, but this one is really good." And then they go back for a second helping! Maxim: You can fool some of the girls some of the time, but you can't fool a man into taking a second helping of something he doesn't really like.

JELLIED FRUITS IN MELON

To serve 6 to 8

1 *large honeydew melon*

1 *(3-ounce) package lime-flavored gelatin*

1 *cup boiling water*

1 *cup fruit syrup and water*

1 *cup canned fruit*

Cut slice off the top of the melon. Scoop out seeds and drain upside down on a plate. Stir boiling water into gelatin mix, dissolving gelatin completely. Drain syrup from canned fruit into measuring cup. Add water until it measures 1 cup. Stir syrup-water into gelatin. Place mixture in refrigerator until it is chilled to a syrupy consistency. Stir in canned fruit and fill melon cavity with the mixture. Replace top and refrigerate for several hours until gelatin is firm. Slice horizontally into 2-inch circles and serve flat on a bed of lettuce.

WALDORF SALAD MOLD

To serve 6 to 8

1 *(6-ounce) package raspberry-flavored gelatin*

2 *cups boiling water*

1 *(16-ounce) can crushed pineapple, drained*

1½ *cups pineapple juice and water*

2 *apples, diced with skin on*

1 *cup broken walnuts*

Empty contents of gelatin package into a deep bowl. Add boiling water and stir until gelatin is completely dissolved. Drain juice from crushed pineapple and add water to make 1½ cups; stir into the gelatin mixture. Add crushed pineapple, diced apples, and walnuts. Lightly oil a 1½-quart fancy mold. Pour gelatin mixture into mold and refrigerate for several hours until firm. Unmold and serve as part of a buffet supper or as a salad course.

CARROT–PINEAPPLE PIE MOLD

To serve 6 to 8

1 *(3-ounce) package lemon-flavored gelatin*
1 *cup boiling water*
½ *cup cold water*
1 *(8-ounce) can pineapple rings with juice*
½ *green pepper*
1 *cup grated fresh carrot*

Empty contents of gelatin package into a bowl. Add boiling water and stir until gelatin is completely dissolved. Add cold water and stir. Add juice from can of pineapple rings. Lightly oil a 10-inch glass pie pan. Pour in ½ inch of gelatin mixture. Arrange pineapple rings equally around pie pan. Place strips of green pepper between rings. Refrigerate until set. Meanwhile, stir grated carrot into remaining gelatin. Chop remaining green pepper and add to gelatin. When pineapple rings are set, pour carrot mixture into pie pan and return to refrigerator until firm. To serve, unmold on a platter of fresh greens and cut in wedges, including part of the pineapple and a strip of green pepper in each serving. This makes a lovely centerpiece for a small dinner party, and may be served with the main course as a side dish.

MANDARIN SHERBET MOLD

To serve 6 to 8

1 *(6-ounce) package orange-flavored gelatin*
1 *cup boiling water*
1 *cup orange juice plus water*
1 *(16-ounce) can Mandarin orange segments*
1 *pint orange sherbet*

Empty contents of gelatin package into a deep bowl. Add boiling water and stir until gelatin is completely dissolved. Drain juice from orange segments and add water to make 1 cup; stir into the gelatin mixture. Add orange segments. Add softened orange sherbet and mix thoroughly. Lightly oil a 1½-quart fancy mold. Pour gelatin mixture into mold and refrigerate for several hours until firm. Unmold and serve as part of a buffet supper or as a salad course.

AMBROSIA RING

To serve 6 to 8

1 *(6-ounce) package orange–pineapple-flavored gelatin*
1 *cup boiling water*
1 *(16-ounce) can crushed pineapple with juice*
2 *(11-ounce) cans Mandarin orange sections with juice*
1 *cup flaked coconut*
1 *pint dairy sour cream*

Empty contents of gelatin package into a deep bowl. Add boiling water and stir until gelatin is completely dissolved. Add crushed pineapple with its juice. Add Mandarin orange sections and juice. Add flaked coconut. Whip sour cream until it is fluffy; add to gelatin mixture. Lightly oil a 2-quart fancy mold. Pour gelatin mixture into mold and refrigerate for several hours until firm. Unmold and serve as part of a buffet supper or as a salad course.

PINEAPPLE–CUCUMBER MOLD

To serve 6 to 8

1 *(6-ounce) package lime-flavored gelatin*
1 *cup boiling water*
1 *(16-ounce) can crushed pineapple with juice*
1 *pint dairy sour cream*
1 *cucumber, chopped coarsely*

Empty contents of gelatin package into a deep bowl. Add boiling water and stir until gelatin is completely dissolved. Add crushed pineapple with its juice. Whip sour cream until it is fluffy; add to gelatin mixture. Add chopped cucumber. Lightly oil a 1½-quart fancy mold. Pour gelatin mixture into mold and refrigerate for several hours until firm. Unmold and serve as part of a buffet supper or as a salad course.

VEGETABLE SALAD MOLD

To serve 6 to 8

1 *(6-ounce) package lemon-flavored gelatin*
1 *tablespoon salt*
2 *cups boiling water*
1½ *cups cold water*
2 *tablespoons vinegar*
1½ *cups finely shredded carrots*
1½ *cups finely shredded cabbage*
1½ *cups finely chopped spinach*
1 *teaspoon minced chives*

Empty contents of gelatin package into a large bowl. Add salt and boiling water and stir until gelatin is completely dissolved. Add cold water and vinegar. Add carrots, cabbage, spinach, and chives. Pour into a lightly oiled 2-quart fancy mold. Refrigerate until firm. Serve as part of a buffet or as a salad course.

BEET SALAD JELL

A QUICK-TRICK WAY

To serve 4 to 6

1 *(3-ounce) package unflavored gelatin*
1 *(1-pound) can julienne beets*
1 *(10½-ounce) can consomme*
½ *cup chopped onion*
1 *tablespoon sugar*
2 *tablespoons lemon juice*
2 *tablespoons dairy sour cream (optional)*

Drain beet juice into bowl. Sprinkle gelatin into beet liquid and stir until it is dissolved. Pour consomme into a saucepan; add onions and simmer for 10 minutes over very low heat. Add gelatin mixture, sugar, lemon juice, and julienne beets to consomme; mix well. Pour into a small flat pan and chill in refrigerator for several hours until firm. Serve in squares on salad greens, with dollops of sour cream.

TOMATO ASPIC

A QUICK-TRICK WAY

To serve 4 to 6

1 *(10-ounce) can tomato juice*
1 *(3-ounce) package lemon-flavored gelatin*
1½ *tablespoons lemon juice*
½ *teaspoon salt*
Dash of pepper

Bring 1 cup tomato juice to a boil. Stir in gelatin until dissolved.
Then pour into tomato juice can, blending with remaining juice.
Stir in lemon juice, salt, and pepper. Chill until firm. To unmold,
puncture bottom of can before dipping in warm water and sliding
gelatin out. Serve as a relish or side salad.

COLE SLAW GELATIN RING

To serve 6 to 8

1 *(3-ounce) package lime-flavored gelatin*
½ *teaspoon salt*
1 *cup boiling water*
2 *tablespoons vinegar*
½ *cup cold water*
½ *cup mayonnaise*
½ *cup dairy sour cream*
1 *teaspoon grated onion*
1 *tablespoon prepared mustard*
1 *teaspoon sugar*
3 *cups shredded cabbage*
2 *tablespoons pimiento*
1 *tablespoon parsley*

Empty contents of gelatin package into a large bowl. Add salt
and boiling water and stir until gelatin is completely dissolved.
Add vinegar and cold water and stir. Add remaining ingredients
and stir well. Lightly oil a 1½-quart ring mold; pour gelatin
mixture into mold and refrigerate until firm. To serve, unmold
on a platter of fresh greens. Serve as part of a buffet supper or
as a salad course.

SHRIMP SALAD MOLD

To serve 4 to 6

1 *envelope unflavored gelatin*
1 *tablespoon lemon juice*
⅓ *cup boiling water*
1 *(8-ounce) can tomato sauce with cheese*
½ *cup dairy sour cream*
½ *cup mayonnaise*
2 *cups cleaned, cooked shrimp*
1 *(9-ounce) package frozen artichoke hearts, cooked and drained*
1 *(4½-ounce) can sliced ripe olives, drained*
½ *teaspoon basil*
Avocado slices (optional)

Soften gelatin in lemon juice; add boiling water and stir until dissolved. Blend in tomato sauce with cheese, sour cream, and mayonnaise. Fold in shrimp, artichoke hearts, olives, and basil. Pour into a 1½-quart mold. Chill until set. Unmold on a chilled serving plate. Garnish with lettuce and slices of avocado, if desired.

WILD RICE AND CHICKEN SALAD MOLD

To serve 8

1 *(6-ounce) package Uncle Ben's White and Wild Rice*
2 *cups cooked, diced chicken*
⅔ *cup chopped green pepper*
¾ *cup diced celery*
⅓ *cup chopped pimiento*
2 *hard-cooked eggs, diced*
1 *tablespoon unflavored gelatin*
1 *cup chicken broth*
2 *teaspoons salt*
1 *tablespoon lemon juice*
⅓ *cup mayonnaise*
⅓ *cup creamy French dressing*
2 *tablespoons Worcestershire sauce*

Cook rice as directed on package. Combine cooked rice, diced chicken, green pepper, celery, pimiento, and diced eggs. Soak gelatin in chicken broth until soft; heat and stir until gelatin is completely dissolved. Combine gelatin solution, salt, lemon juice, mayonnaise, French dressing, and Worcestershire sauce and add to the salad ingredients. Mix well. Pour into a lightly oiled 1½-quart mold. Chill until firm. Unmold and serve as a luncheon main dish, as part of a buffet, or as a salad course at dinner.

❧ 15 ❧

It's All Gravy

WHAT'S THE DIFFERENCE BETWEEN SLICED FILET MIGNON AND Chateaubriand? Gravy! And it's the ability to make the sauce that separates the girls from the cooks.

So you've learned how to broil a steak, poach a fish, and roast a turkey. These are certainly important skills, and you are well on your way to being appreciated for life; but learn to smother each of these dishes in gravy for a juicier, tastier offering and you will earn compliments that you had never dreamed possible. Feeding ends and dining begins with a simple turn of the gravy ladle.

A while back, I remember being appalled by a friend who had roasted a turkey to perfection but who had made a deal with the corner delicatessen for the purchase of a quart of turkey gravy. She said that she simply could not make the gravy herself. Is that really possible? She had the pan with the turkey drippings for a marvelous start. All she had to do was to add boiling water to the roasting pan and scrape and stir it around with a wire whisk or slotted spoon as it simmered over a low flame. A little salt and pepper would have answered the flavoring problem, and a chicken bouillon cube would do wonders. A tablespoon or so of cornstarch mixed with a few tablespoons of cold water to prevent lumping and then whisked through the gravy (stirring constantly while cooking it) would have thickened the mixture and still produced a clear-looking product. If she didn't mind opaque gravy, she could have used flour instead. If the gravy was not thick enough, she could have added some more thickening agent, stirring until the mixture reached the boiling point and the desired thickness. Remember, when you are making gravy, to add cold liquid to a thickening agent before stirring it into hot liquid. If the color looks pale and wan, add a dash of prepared Gravy Master and stir briskly. Season the gravy until it has a piquant flavor of its own. Serve piping hot.

In this chapter, I have also included traditional recipes for sauces, for I feel that you should master the art of making these delicious additions which complement so many dishes. However, there are also marvelous mixes available in your market; they will allow you to use shortcuts when you must. One mix that I am particularly fond of is a hollandaise mix. The simple addition of water will turn it into a reasonable facsimile of the real thing in a matter of seconds. What a difference the prepared sauce makes to a dish of plain broccoli. The lemony tang lifts the vegetable from the realm of a good-for-you green vegetable to a heavenly offering.

Once you develop the skill of turning pan drippings into toothsome gravy, and a start-from-scratch roux of butter and flour into a fine sauce, your meals will never be dull fare. Even the saucy tricks for desserts at the end of the chapter will encourage you to shine up your ladle and dip up more compliments.

PAN GRAVY

A QUICK-TRICK WAY

To make 2 cups of gravy
2 tablespoons flour
¼ cup pan drippings from roast
1½ cups boiling water
¼ teaspoon salt
⅛ teaspoon pepper
1 tablespoon Gravy Master (optional)

Stir flour into pan drippings and brown over low heat. Stir in boiling water, and stir constantly until mixture has cooked for several minutes. Add salt and pepper. If you desire a richer brown color, add a tablespoon of commercial Gravy Master.

BURGUNDY–MUSHROOM GRAVY

A QUICK-TRICK WAY

To make 2 cups of gravy
1 *(3-ounce) can sliced mushrooms*
½ *cup Burgundy wine*
2 *tablespoons dried onion flakes*
2 *tablespoons dried parsley flakes*
2 *teaspoons Gravy Master*
1 *cup water*
2 *tablespoons flour*

Empty mushrooms into a saucepan. Add Burgundy wine, onion flakes, parsley flakes, Gravy Master, and water. Simmer for 5 minutes. Mix flour with enough cold water to make a thin paste. Spoon some hot gravy mixture into the cold flour mixture, stir, and pour flour paste into the hot gravy mixture. Simmer and stir constantly until mixture is thickened and cooked for about 3 minutes. Serve this delicious sauce poured over a thick broiled steak.

POLYNESIAN BARBECUE SAUCE

To make 1½ cups of sauce
1 *(8-ounce) can tomato sauce*
½ *cup apricot preserves*
1 *teaspoon soy sauce*
1 *teaspoon brown sugar*
1 *teaspoon minced onion*
1 *teaspoon prepared mustard*
½ *teaspoon salt*
¼ *teaspoon monosodium glutamate*
⅛ *teaspoon ginger*

Empty tomato sauce into a saucepan. Add apricot preserves. Add remaining ingredients, stirring well. Simmer for 10 minutes. Use this sauce to baste spareribs or chicken parts while roasting.

WHITE WINE–MUSHROOM GRAVY

A QUICK-TRICK WAY

To make 1½ cups of gravy
1 *(10½-ounce) can chicken consomme*
1 *(4-ounce) can sliced mushrooms*
2 *tablespoons dried onion flakes*
2 *tablespoons Gravy Master*
½ *cup white wine*
2 *tablespoons lemon juice*
2 *tablespoons flour*
¼ *cup cold water*

Empty the can of consomme into a saucepan. Add mushrooms. Add onion flakes, Gravy Master, white wine, and lemon juice. Simmer for several minutes. Stir flour and cold water together until smooth. Slowly add this to the gravy mixture, then continue to stir until the mixture reaches the boiling point and thickens. Pour over slices of chicken and serve hot.

VELOUTÉ SAUCE

To make 1 cup of sauce
2 *tablespoons butter*
2 *tablespoons flour*
1 *cup chicken consomme*
¼ *teaspoon salt*
Dash of pepper

Melt butter in a saucepan and add flour. Stir in chicken consomme, salt, and pepper. Cook until thickened, stirring constantly. Serve as topping for poultry, hot cooked fish, eggs, or vegetables.

ALMOND BUTTER SAUCE

To make ¾ cup of sauce
½ *cup butter*
1 *tablespoon lemon juice*
¼ *cup slivered almonds*

133

Melt butter in a saucepan. Remove from heat. Stir in lemon juice and slivered almonds. Delicious with broiled fish.

RAISIN SAUCE

To make 1½ cups sauce
½ cup red wine
½ cup water
¼ cup sugar
½ teaspoon dry mustard
¼ teaspoon ground cloves
¼ cup seedless raisins

In a saucepan, combine wine, water, sugar, mustard, and ground cloves. Heat together for 3 minutes. Add raisins; simmer for 15 minutes, stirring occasionally. This sauce may be used on ham or tongue slices.

WHITE SAUCE

To make 1 cup of sauce

THIN SAUCE:	MEDIUM SAUCE:	THICK SAUCE:
1 tbsp. butter	2 tbsp. butter	3 tbsp. butter
1 tbsp. flour	2 tbsp. flour	3 tbsp. flour
1 cup milk	1 cup milk	1 cup milk
¼ tsp. salt	¼ tsp. salt	¼ tsp. salt
Dash of pepper	Dash of pepper	Dash of pepper

Melt butter in a saucepan and stir in flour. Add milk gradually, stirring constantly until mixture is thickened. Add salt and pepper. Cook 3 to 4 minutes in all. Use this as a basic cream sauce for vegetables.

Add grated cheese, hard-cooked egg slices, or fresh chopped dill to vary the flavor.

HOLLANDAISE SAUCE
A QUICK-TRICK WAY

To make ½ cup sauce	*To make 1 cup sauce*
2 egg yolks	4 egg yolks
2 tablespoons lemon juice	¼ cup lemon juice

| Dash of salt | ⅛ teaspoon salt |
| ⅓ cup sweet butter, melted | ⅔ cup sweet butter, melted |

Warm the jar of an electric blender with hot water; empty completely. Be sure butter is melted before you start as this method requires fast movements. Quick-blend egg yolks, lemon juice, and salt. Slowly add melted butter in a steady stream. Turn blender off when the last drop of butter is added. Serve on asparagus, broccoli, or Eggs Benedict (see page 36).

SEAFOOD COCKTAIL SAUCE

To make 1 cup of sauce
½ cup tomato catsup
⅓ cup chili sauce
1 tablespoon prepared horseradish
1 tablespoon lemon juice

Combine tomato catsup and chili sauce, mixing well. Add horseradish and lemon juice. Chill until serving time.

HOMEMADE FRENCH DRESSING

A QUICK-TRICK WAY

To make about 3 cups of dressing
1 (10½-ounce) can condensed tomato soup
¼ cup sugar
1 cup vinegar
½ cup salad oil
1 onion, diced
1 clove garlic, peeled
1 teaspoon salt
1 teaspoon dry mustard
1 teaspoon Worcestershire sauce
¼ teaspoon pepper

Place all ingredients in an electric blender. Blend to a smooth sauce. Refrigerate. May be stored in refrigerator for several weeks in a tightly closed container.

MARSHMALLOW DRESSING

A QUICK-TRICK WAY

To make 2 cups of dressing
1 *cup sour cream*
1 *cup marshmallows, cut up*

To make 4 cups of dressing
1 *pint sour cream*
2 *cups marshmallows, cut up*

Combine sour cream and marshmallows in a large jar with a tight cover. Refrigerate overnight. Then beat until smooth at medium speed in an electric mixer or blender. Refrigerate and use on fruit salads or fancy gelatin molds.

BLUEBERRY SAUCE

To make 2 cups of sauce
1 *cup fresh blueberries*
½ *cup water*
⅓ *cup sugar*
1 *teaspoon cornstarch*
⅛ *teaspoon salt*
1 *teaspoon butter*
2 *tablespoons lemon juice*

Combine ½ cup blueberries and water in a saucepan and bring to a boil; reduce heat and simmer for 3 minutes. Combine sugar, cornstarch, and salt; stir mixture into hot berries. Simmer and stir until thick and clear. Add remaining berries, butter, and lemon juice. Stir until butter is melted, then remove at once from heat. Serve warm or cold on slices of sponge cake, pound cake, or angel food cake. Enough for 6 to 8 slices.

LEMON-CUSTARD CAKE SAUCE

To make 2 cups of sauce
3 *egg yolks*
¼ *cup sugar*
1 *teaspoon grated lemon peel*
¼ *cup lemon juice*
1 *cup heavy cream, whipped*
2 *drops yellow food coloring*

Beat egg yolks with sugar until light. Blend in lemon peel and juice. Cook in the top of a double boiler over hot—not boiling—water, stirring constantly until smooth and thick, adding the yellow food coloring. Cool completely. Fold into whipped cream. Serve over slices of angel food or sponge cake. Enough for 6 to 8 slices.

CHOCOLATE FUDGE SAUCE

A QUICK-TRICK WAY

To make 1 cup of sauce
1 *(6-ounce) package semisweet chocolate bits*
½ cup evaporated milk

In the top of a double boiler, over hot water, melt chocolate bits. Stir in evaporated milk until well blended. Serve warm over ice cream. May be refrigerated and reheated over hot water.

❧ 16 ❧

A Treasury of Desserts

WHY ARE SOME WOMEN GREAT BAKERS WHILE OTHERS REGARD baking as a mysterious rite to be performed only by the specially blessed? Behind every reputation for baking talent is usually a small group of tested recipes which are proven winners.

When you find a brownie recipe that has the degree of chewiness you prefer, is rich with chocolate flavor, and has clear directions that produce perfection every time—when you honestly feel that these brownies are the best you've ever tasted—write the recipe on a card and put it into your permanent "winners file."

This is the method which makes the reputation of a good baker. The secret is to search for a good recipe, and once you find it, to stick with it until you discover a better one to take its place. To start you on your way, a good collection of tried and tested recipes is included in this chapter. They are not labeled beginners' recipes, because there is no beginning or end to good food and good taste. Either it is good or it isn't.

In addition to the start-from-scratch cake recipes, you will find a group of quick-tricks that make use of store-bought layer cakes, packaged cake mixes, and dessert mixes used ingeniously so that they appear to be homemade.

To facilitate your baking, keep a few emergency trimmings on hand—a small can of grated coconut, squares of unsweetened chocolate for grating, a can of walnut halves, and several packages of assorted frosting mixes.

It is not enough to know *what* to do when baking cakes; you should also know *why* and *how* you do it. Scores of books have been written on baking, but our aim here is to provide simple and clear definitions of the basic baking procedures.

Beating is done with an electric mixer, a rotary beater, a wire whisk, or a wooden spoon with plenty of arm power behind it. The object is to whip air into the mixture.

Creaming is the blending together of two or more ingredients into a new-textured, fluffy mixture. This can be done with an electric mixer or the back of a large wooden spoon.

Folding is an under–over technique, best accomplished with a large spatula or spoon, which gently turns the mixture from top to bottom to blend the ingredients together without a loss of air.

Remove your eggs, butter, or cream cheese from the refrigerator and have them at room temperature before you start to combine ingredients for a cake. Before you begin to assemble the rest of the ingredients, preheat the oven to the temperature recommended for the recipe. Allow at least fifteen minutes for the oven to adjust to the required heat. Don't start any procedure until you have gathered all of the recipe ingredients and have the necessary implements in front of you.

Grease the bottom of the cake pan with melted butter applied with a pastry brush. Dust with flour and tap out the excess flour that does not stick to the butter. Unless otherwise specified in the recipe, do not grease the sides of the pan or the batter will have difficulty climbing up the slippery sides. No matter what order of procedure is given in the recipe, sift the dry ingredients first and set them aside. This will prevent loss of air in the batter, which will occur if you take the time to do this step in any other sequence.

If the recipe calls for separated eggs, hold each egg over a small deep bowl and crack the egg sharply across the middle with a dull knife. As the white of the egg drains into the bowl below, slip the yolk from one shell half to the other, helping to drain the remaining egg white without breaking the yolk. Slip the unbroken yolk into a waiting bowl. A few grains of salt will increase the volume of beaten egg whites.

Now for a few *don'ts* which everyone learns from experience or from a teacher. *Don't* open the oven door to peek in while the cake is baking, except near the very end of the recommended baking time. *Don't* open the oven door at all if you are baking a cheese cake, at least not until one hour after you have turned off the heat. *Don't* try to bake on both racks at the same time; nothing will turn out properly in an overcrowded oven. *Don't* hesitate to insert a wooden toothpick to test if the cake is underdone. (If the toothpick comes out with clinging moist batter, bake the cake for a few more moments.) *Don't* forget to set a timer to remind you when to take the cake out of the oven. And *don't* worry if you have a few fiascos; they happen in the happiest of kitchens!

CREAM CHEESE PIE PASTRY

To make a 1-crust, 9-inch pie
4 ounces cream cheese
4 ounces butter
1 cup flour

To make a 2-crust, 9-inch pie
8 ounces cream cheese
8 ounces butter
2 cups flour

Blend the cream cheese and butter together. (It will be easier if they are left at room temperature an hour before used.) Add flour and work into a smooth dough. Refrigerate for several hours before rolling. For a 2-crust pie, divide dough in half and roll out 1 portion on a floured board for bottom crust. Repeat for top crust. Use for Apple Pie (see page 141), or fill with canned pie filling, following directions on can for preparation and baking.

For a 1-crust pie, roll out dough as above. Place loosely in pie pan, prick unbaked crust with fork every few inches, and bake at 350 degrees for 20 minutes, or until browned. Use for Pecan Pie (see page 141), or fill with prepared pie filling from a convenience food mix. Top with whipped cream.

You will find this dough easy to roll and handle, and it has a delicious flavor. Scraps of leftover dough may be rolled out, cut with the floured rim of a small glass, and baked on a cookie sheet at 350 degrees until edges are browned.

APPLE PIE

To make a 9-inch pie
1 *(2-crust) Cream Cheese Pie Pastry (see page 140)*
2 *pounds tart apples*
⅔ *cup sugar*
2 *teaspoons lemon juice*
2 *tablespoons cornstarch*
½ *teaspoon cinnamon*
¼ *teaspoon nutmeg*
2 *tablespoons butter*
American cheese (optional)

Core, peel, and slice apples. Add sugar, lemon juice, cornstarch, cinnamon, and nutmeg. Fill unbaked pastry crust with half the apple mixture. Dot with half the butter. Fill with remaining apple mixture and dot with remaining butter. Cover with top crust, sealing edges well. Prick top with a fork in several places to let steam escape. Paint top of crust with milk. Bake at 425 degrees for about 40 minutes, or until crust is browned to a golden color. Serve hot or cold, with a slice of American cheese if desired.

PECAN PIE

To make a 9-inch pie
1 *(1-crust) Cream Cheese Pie Pastry (see page 140)*
1 *cup pecan halves*
4 *eggs*
1 *cup dark corn syrup*
½ *cup sugar*
¼ *cup butter, melted*
1 *teaspoon vanilla*

Arrange pecan halves over the bottom surface of the pie crust Beat eggs. Add corn syrup. Add sugar, melted butter, and vanilla Beat well. Pour mixture into pecan-lined pie crust. Bake in a 350-degree oven for 1 hour. Cool before serving.

CHOCOLATE BROWNIES

To make about 2 dozen brownies

4 *eggs*

2 *cups sugar*

¾ *cup butter*

4 *squares unsweetened baking chocolate*

1½ *cups flour*

1 *teaspoon baking powder*

1 *teaspoon vanilla*

1 *cup broken walnuts*

½ *cup seedless raisins (optional)*

Beat eggs. Add sugar gradually, beating well. In the top of a double boiler, melt butter and chocolate together; add to egg mixture. Sift flour and baking powder; add gradually to batter, beating well. Add vanilla. Add walnuts and raisins. Pour into a lightly greased 9-inch-by-13-inch flat baking pan. Bake at 350 degrees for about 25 minutes. Remove from oven and cool. Cut into 2-inch squares.

CREAM CHEESE POUND CAKE

To serve 12

3 *ounces cream cheese*

¼ *pound butter*

1 *cup sugar*

3 *eggs*

1 *cup flour, sifted*

1 *teaspoon baking powder*

1 *teaspoon vanilla*

1 *tablespoon grated lemon rind*

With an electric mixer or hand beater, mix cream cheese and butter together. Add sugar and cream well into a fluffy texture. Add eggs, 1 at a time. Turn mixer to low speed and add flour and baking powder a little at a time. When thoroughly blended into mixture, add vanilla and grated lemon rind. Grease and flour lightly an 8-inch-by-4-inch loaf pan. Scrape batter into loaf pan and bake at 350 degrees for 50 to 60 minutes, until top is lightly browned. Remove from oven and cool at room temperature. May be kept for several days in the refrigerator; also freezes well for several months.

CHEESE CAKE

To serve 12

6 *eggs, separated*
1 *pound cream cheese*
1 *pint dairy sour cream*
1 *cup sugar*
3 *tablespoons flour*
1 *teaspoon vanilla*
3 *tablespoons lemon juice*
Strawberry Glaze (optional, see page 145)

Preheat oven to 300 degrees. With an electric mixer or a hand beater, beat egg yolks until lemon-colored. Mash cream cheese in a separate bowl until soft; add to egg yolks and beat through. Add sour cream and beat through. Turn mixer to low speed and add sugar and flour. Beat thoroughly, then add vanilla and lemon juice. In a separate bowl, with clean beaters, beat egg whites until soft peaks form. Fold the thick whites through the batter with a large spoon, using a slow under–over stroke to combine the batters without losing aeration. Pour batter into a 10-inch springform pan. Bake at 300 degrees for 1 hour; turn off oven and let cake cool in the oven for 2 hours before removing it. If desired, top with Strawberry Glaze. When cake is completely cooled, refrigerate it until serving. To serve, remove outer springform, leaving cake on the pan base.

APPLE STRUDEL

A QUICK-TRICK WAY

To serve 6 to 8

DOUGH:

1 *cup flour*
1 *egg*
¼ *pound butter*

1 *(16-ounce) can apple pie slices*
½ *cup orange marmalade*
½ *cup raisins*
½ *cup shredded coconut*
1 *tablespoon brown sugar*

Put flour in a bowl; add the egg and butter. Work into a dough with your hands or with a pastry cutter. Refrigerate the dough for 1 hour. Then roll out dough on a floured pastry board into a rectangle about 6 by 12 inches. Combine canned apples, orange marmalade, raisins, coconut, and brown sugar. Spread this filling along the length of the dough, allowing 2 inches on each side and 1 inch on each end to remain uncovered. Fold 1 long side of dough over filling. Fold both ends over. Then fold other long side over and press or pinch dough together to seal in the filling. Place in a shallow ungreased pan. Bake in a 350-degree oven for 1 hour, or until pastry is golden. Can be served hot or cold.

ORANGE SPONGE CAKE

To serve 12
6 *eggs, separated*
1½ *cups sugar*
½ *cup orange juice*
1 *tablespoon lemon juice*
1½ *cups flour*
1½ *teaspoons baking powder*
½ *teaspoon salt*

With an electric mixer or hand beater, beat egg yolks until lemon-colored. Add sugar; beat well. Add orange juice and lemon juice; beat well. Sift flour, baking powder, and salt together. Beat slowly into the batter. In a separate bowl, with clean beaters, beat egg whites until stiff. Fold whites into batter with a large spoon, using careful over-and-under motions to combine the ingredients without loss of aeration. Bake in an ungreased 10-inch tube pan for 35 minutes in a 325-degree oven. Surface should be golden brown and spring back when gently touched. Remove from oven and invert immediately on a cake rack, or place upside down with funnel on a soda bottle. Cool for at least an hour before removing from pan.

STRAWBERRY GLAZE

To glaze 1 large cake
1 *pint whole strawberries, fresh or frozen*
¾ *cup sugar*
¼ *cup cold water*
1½ *tablespoons cornstarch*
1 *teaspoon butter*
3 *drops red food coloring*

Arrange clean whole strawberries around the top of the cake, reserving about ⅔ cup for the glaze. Crush the reserved berries and place in a small saucepan. Add sugar, water, and cornstarch; stir until cornstarch is completely dissolved. Cook over medium heat, stirring constantly, until mixture begins to boil. Add butter and red food coloring, stirring through thoroughly. Spoon hot mixture over whole berries on top of cake, carefully covering both the berries and top surface of cake. Chill until serving time.

SOUR CREAM COFFEE CAKE

To serve 12
¾ *cup butter*
1¼ *cups sugar*
2 *eggs, beaten*
1 *cup dairy sour cream*
1 *teaspoon vanilla*
2 *cups flour*
1 *teaspoon baking powder*
½ *teaspoon baking soda*

TOPPING:
¾ *cup chopped nuts*
¼ *cup sugar*
1 *teaspoon cinnamon*
Confectioners' sugar

Preheat oven to 350 degrees. Cream butter and sugar together with an electric mixer or hand beater. Add beaten eggs. Add sour cream. Add vanilla, beating well after each addition. Sift flour, baking powder, and baking soda into a separate bowl. Turn mixer to low speed and add flour mixture gradually until it is well mixed into the batter. Lightly grease a 10-inch tube pan and pour half the batter into it. Combine the topping ingredients: nuts, sugar, and cinnamon. Sprinkle half of the topping mixture over the batter in the tube pan, pour remaining batter over this, and top with the remaining topping mixture. Bake for 55 to 60 minutes at 350 degrees. Remove from oven and while still hot sprinkle with confectioners' sugar.

TORTE ANGELIQUE

A QUICK-TRICK WAY

To serve 8
1 bakery 8-inch angel food cake
1 package instant chocolate pudding
1 pint heavy whipping cream
1 square baking chocolate

Cut cake into 3 layers. Mix instant chocolate pudding with cream. Let mixture stand until pudding is dissolved; then whip, being careful not to overwhip. Stop the instant the cream is perfectly whipped. Spread mixture between layers and over outside of cake. Hold a grater over the top of the cake and grate the baking chocolate for a delicious decorative effect. Place in freezing compartment or in refrigerator turned to its coldest degree for several hours before serving.

PUDDING POUND CAKE

A QUICK-TRICK WAY

To serve 10 to 12
1 package yellow cake mix
½ cup vegetable oil
1 cup milk
4 eggs
1 package instant lemon pudding

Empty yellow cake mix into a mixing bowl. Add oil, milk, and eggs; beat thoroughly for 3 minutes. Add instant pudding to the batter; beat 1 minute more. Grease an angel food tube pan; pour in batter. Bake at 350 degrees for 45 to 55 minutes. Remove from oven and cool.

LEMON WAFERS

To make 2 dozen cookies
1½ *tablespoons butter*
½ *cup sugar*
1 *egg*
1 *teaspoon lemon extract*
¾ *cup flour*
⅛ *teaspoon salt*
1 *teaspoon baking powder*
3 *tablespoons milk*

Cream butter and sugar together. Beat in egg and lemon extract. Sift flour, salt, and baking powder together; add alternately with milk to batter, beating well. Drop half teaspoonfuls about 2 inches apart on a greased baking sheet. Bake in a 350-degree oven for 10 to 15 minutes, or until wafers have a brown edge. Remove from oven and cool.

COCONUT MACAROONS

To make 2 dozen cookies
2 *egg whites*
Dash of salt
½ *teaspoon vanilla*
⅔ *cup sugar*
1⅓ *cups flaked coconut*

Beat egg whites with salt until soft peaks form. Add vanilla and gradually add sugar, beating whites until stiff. Fold in coconut. Drop by rounded teaspoonfuls on a greased cookie sheet. Bake in a 325-degree oven for 20 minutes. Remove from oven. Store cookies in a tightly closed canister.

MARBLE SOUR CREAM CAKE RING

To serve 10 to 12

¼ *cup cocoa*

1¼ *cups sugar*

¼ *cup boiling water*

¼ *pound butter*

2 *eggs, beaten*

1 *teaspoon vanilla*

2 *cups flour*

1 *teaspoon baking powder*

¼ *teaspoon salt*

¼ *cup milk*

¾ *cup dairy sour cream*

Mix cocoa and ¼ cup sugar into boiling water; stir until dissolved and set aside to cool. Meanwhile, cream butter and 1 cup sugar together until fluffy. Add beaten eggs. Add vanilla. Sift flour, baking powder, and salt together. Stir together milk and sour cream. Then alternately add the flour mixture and the sour cream mixture to the batter until all is mixed well. Pour half of the batter into a greased 10-inch tube pan. Stir the cocoa mixture into the remaining half of the batter; then drop by tablespoonfuls onto plain batter in the pan. With a knife, zigzag through the batter once, creating a rippled appearance of chocolate through the vanilla batter. Bake in a 350-degree over for 40 minutes.

MOCHA REFRIGERATOR CAKE

To serve 6

6 *ounces semisweet chocolate*

2 *tablespoons strong coffee (instant coffee may be used)*

4 *eggs, separated*

½ *teaspoon vanilla*

18 *ladyfingers, split lengthwise*

½ *pint heavy cream, whipped*

In the top of a double boiler, over hot water, melt chocolate. Add coffee, and stir well. Remove from heat. Add yolks of eggs one at a time, beating vigorously. Add vanilla. Cool. Beat the egg whites stiff. Fold into chocolate mixture, using an under–over stroke, being careful not to lose aeration. Lightly butter a 9-inch-by-4½-inch loaf pan; stand ladyfinger halves around edges and place a layer across bottom of pan. Pour in half the chocolate mixture. Place another layer of ladyfinger halves over batter; top with remaining chocolate mixture and then remaining ladyfinger halves. Cover with foil and chill for several hours or overnight. Unmold just before serving and top with whipped cream.

POTS DE CRÈME

To serve 6
2 ounces semisweet chocolate
¼ cup sugar
1½ cups heavy cream
6 egg yolks
1 teaspoon vanilla
Whipped cream (optional)

Melt chocolate in the top of a double boiler over hot water. Add sugar and stir until dissolved. Add heavy cream and stir until blended and smooth. Beat egg yolks lightly and add to chocolate mixture. Add vanilla. Pour into 6 individual china pots or small sherbet glasses. Cover with foil, and refrigerate until serving time. Serve with a dollop of whipped cream, if desired.

ICE CREAM BOMBE WITH STRAWBERRY SAUCE

To serve 6 to 8
1 quart coffee ice cream
1 pint butter pecan ice cream
1 (8-ounce) package frozen strawberries
2 tablespoons sugar
1 teaspoon lemon juice

Soften ice cream until it can be spooned easily into a 1½-quart fancy fluted mold. First spoon the coffee ice cream into the mold and push it to the sides, leaving a large well in the center. Fill center with the butter pecan ice cream. Cover top of mold with foil and return to freezer until ready to use. Two hours before serving, thaw strawberries. When thawed, stir in sugar and lemon juice until completely dissolved. Remove ice cream from mold by dipping pan up to rim in warm water for a moment and then turning out on an attractive serving dish. Pour strawberry sauce over the top and serve immediately.

BAKED APPLE AMBROSIA

For each serving

1 *apple*

1 *teaspoon brown sugar*

¼ *teaspoon cinnamon*

2 *teaspoons raisins*

1 *teaspoon grated coconut*

½ *teaspoon butter*

Pare the skin from each apple about ⅓ of the way down from the top. Core the apple. Fill each core with mixture of brown sugar, cinnamon, raisins, grated coconut, and butter. Place in a pan with enough water to cover the bottom of the pan. Bake in a 350-degree oven for 1 hour, or until tender. Serve hot or cold.

HOT FRUIT COMPOTE

A QUICK-TRICK WAY

To serve 6 to 8

1 *(16-ounce) can peach halves*

1 *(16-ounce) can pear halves*

1 *(16-ounce) can apricot halves*

½ *teaspoon cinnamon*

1 *tablespoon lemon juice*

½ *cup red wine*

In a saucepan, combine canned fruits with their juices. Add cinnamon, lemon juice, and wine. Simmer for 5 minutes. Pour into warmed fancy bowl. Serve hot in individual fruit dishes at the table.

❧ 17 ❧

Breads with a Twist

You CAN BECOME A PACKAGE-MIX GENIUS WITH A FEW SLEIGHT-of-hand tricks which separate the plodding mix-bakers from the clever users of convenience foods. Ready-to-mix muffin and quick bread products can be given a homemade flair. All it takes is a little ingenuity to transform the mix into something of your own invention.

It is definitely worth your time to become acquainted with the quick bread and muffin mixes on your grocer's food shelves. You will find corn muffins, rye muffins, orange muffins, even delicacies like apricot–nut bread. They can simply be mixed as directed on the package or they can be baked in a mold or loaf. Many can be mixed together to produce a delicious new treat. I urge you to be adventurous and to be alert for new mixes as they appear on the market. To give you an idea of how to use them, I have included some quick-trick ideas for muffin and bread mixes in this chapter.

Besides the varied assortment of available packaged mixes, there are many kinds of refrigerated biscuits and rolls that make an excellent base for other quick-tricks. My favorite is the crescent roll which almost begs for a filling before the triangles are rolled up. A sprinkling of Parmesan cheese, grated cheddar cheese, herbs mashed in butter, or even sugar-and-cinnamon will turn this good product into a great one.

Sometimes the novelty of your bread or muffin offering will be the way you baked it. For example, you may use a muffin mix to produce one giant muffin rather than twelve tiny ones or bake a quick bread mix in a ring mold instead of a loaf pan. Make sure, however, that the mold is not too large for the amount of batter. The batter should reach at least halfway up the pan before baking.

The addition of hot buttered garlic bread to a simple broiled-steak-and-salad dinner makes the menu much more interesting. Buy a fresh loaf of French bread, slit it partially through with a diagonal slice every two inches, and brush a combination of crushed garlic and melted butter over the exposed slices of bread. Wrap the entire long loaf in foil and bake for about ten minutes before serving.

Breads always create a more lasting impression if you serve them on an interesting-looking board or tray, and allow the host to slice away at the table. It is important to inform him beforehand what you are serving and the best method to cut and serve it at the table. A short conference with your husband before the guests arrive will insure his success and eliminate a helpless why-did-you-do-this-to-me? look as he struggles with some unknown breadstuff.

The ideas in this chapter should serve to spark your own inventiveness. Since there are hundreds of food manufacturers vying to make your life easier, this is one area of meal planning for which it pays to listen to the sales pitch!

ORANGE–NUT MUFFINS

A QUICK-TRICK WAY

To make 12 muffins
¼ cup orange marmalade
¼ cup chopped walnuts
1 package orange muffin mix

Grease a muffin tin and spoon 1 teaspoon orange marmalade and 1 teaspoon chopped walnuts into each muffin cup. Mix orange muffin mix according to directions on the box. Fill muffin cups half full, and bake in a 400-degree oven for about 15 minutes. Cool slightly and remove from the muffin cups. Delicious when warm.

ONION–RYE MUFFINS

A QUICK-TRICK WAY

To make 12 muffins
1 *package rye muffin mix*
½ *package dehydrated onion soup mix*

Prepare rye muffin mix batter according to directions on package. Stir in onion soup mix. Bake according to directions on package. Serve warm or cold.

ONION CRESCENTS

A QUICK-TRICK WAY

To make 8 rolls
1 *package refrigerated crescent rolls*
¼ *cup dairy sour cream*
½ *teaspoon onion salt*

Separate rolls and carefully unroll each. Spread each triangle with sour cream and sprinkle with onion salt. Reroll crescents, starting at the widest end. Place on a greased baking sheet. Bake at 375 degrees for 12 to 15 minutes, or until golden brown. Serve warm.

HERBED BUTTER CRESCENTS

A QUICK-TRICK WAY

To make 8 crescents
1 *package refrigerated crescent rolls*
¼ *teaspoon thyme*
¼ *teaspoon marjoram*
2 *tablespoons butter, softened*

Separate rolls and carefully unroll each. Mash thyme and marjoram into softened butter. Spread mixture over each roll. Reroll crescents, starting at the widest end. Place on a greased baking sheet. Bake at 375 degrees for 12 to 15 minutes, or until golden brown. Serve warm.

CORN NIBLET BREAD

A QUICK-TRICK WAY

To make 1 loaf

1 *(12-ounce) package corn bread mix*
1 *cup canned corn niblets, drained*
2 *tablespoons chopped chives*

Follow directions on corn bread mix package to prepare batter. Add drained corn niblets and chopped chives. Bake according to directions on package. Serve warm.

HUSH PUPPIES

A QUICK-TRICK WAY

To make 2 dozen

1 *(12-ounce) package corn bread mix*
1 *tablespoon dehydrated minced onion*
1 *egg*
⅓ *cup beer*
¼ *cup cooking oil*

Combine corn bread mix, onion, egg, and beer. Stir together until well blended. Heat oil in a skillet. Drop corn bread batter by spoonfuls into hot oil and cook for 2 to 3 minutes, or until golden brown. Turn Hush Puppies to brown evenly. Remove with slotted spoon and drain on absorbent paper. Repeat until all are done, adding more oil if necessary. Hush Puppies may be prepared the day before; to reheat, wrap in foil and place in a 350-degree oven for 5 to 6 minutes. Serve hot.

CINNAMON–NUT ROLLS

A QUICK-TRICK WAY

To make 10 rolls

1 *package (10 biscuits) refrigerated biscuits*
¼ *cup brown sugar*
½ *teaspoon cinnamon*
¼ *cup chopped walnuts*
2 *tablespoons melted butter*

154

Separate biscuits; on a lightly floured surface, flatten each biscuit to ⅛-inch thickness. Combine sugar, cinnamon, nuts, and melted butter. Spread each biscuit with this mixture and roll up, jelly-roll fashion. Grease muffin tin and fill each cup with a rolled biscuit by coiling the roll into the muffin cup. Bake in a 400-degree oven for 10 to 15 minutes, until the biscuits are golden. Serve hot.

APRICOT–ORANGE NUT LOAF

A QUICK-TRICK WAY

To make 2 small loaves or 1 large one

1 *package apricot nut bread mix*

1 *package orange bread mix*

1 *tablespoon lemon juice*

Follow directions on packages, mixing each bread separately. When each is thoroughly mixed, stir them together. Add lemon juice. Pour into 2 regular loaf pans or 1 large ring mold, filling containers only halfway with batter. Bake according to directions on the packages. Serve warm or cold.

ORANGE–NUT BREAD

To serve 8

2 *cups flour*

2 *teaspoons baking powder*

½ *teaspoon salt*

½ *cup butter*

1 *cup sugar*

2 *eggs*

2 *tablespoons frozen orange juice concentrate*

¾ *cup milk*

1 *cup chopped walnuts*

Sift flour, baking powder, and salt together. Cream butter and sugar together until fluffy. Add eggs and beat until smooth. Add frozen orange juice concentrate. Alternately add flour mixture and milk, ending with flour; beat until smooth. Add chopped nuts. Pour into a greased loaf pan 9 inches by 4½ inches, and bake for about 1 hour in a 350-degree oven. Remove when lightly browned, and cool. Slice and serve.

❦ 18 ❦

Party Pick-ups

NOTHING GETS A PARTY OFF TO A BETTER START THAN A ... selection of hors d'oeuvres. Palate pleasers will become a conversation piece if two things are kept in mind. First, avoid contrived bits of open sandwiches that dry up too quickly and look like an invitation to ptomaine in an hour. Second, if you have provided some exotic taste-tempters be sure to include some bland ones for your less adventurous guests. Some people are distressed by an array of strange-looking foods with no relief in sight.

Aside from these precautions, imagination and good taste are your only limitations. Dips should not be too drippy but should have a consistency that adheres well to a cracker or chip. Your guests will not appreciate soiled clothing from runny foods.

A wedge of cheese with do-it-yourself crackers will disappear as if mice were on the town. The larger the cheese the more magnetic it becomes. Be sure the knives you use are sturdy enough to do a good cutting and spreading job. There are some ceramic-handled knives that are beautiful to look at, but they will break under the first he-man pressure, leaving your guest feeling annoyed and guilty.

If your appetizers are intended merely to whet the appetite for the dinner to follow, try to limit the selection to two or three things—for instance, a dip with potato chips, a pâté spread, and a platter of fried shrimp with a spicy sauce. Or make the Quiche Lorraine pie in this chapter and serve it alone, using it as a first course, before going to the dinner table. Limit your cocktails and appetizers in relation to the courses you have planned for dinner or else your guests may be too stimulated and satiated to appreciate your culinary efforts.

If the appetizers comprise your entire offering, as for a cocktail party, prepare the kind of food that won't be difficult to manage. Be sure that they are pick-upable, one-bite kinds of things that are easy to handle for a large group of guests. Small napkins, plates, and coasters will help to keep your guests comfortable and your furnishings intact.

In this chapter there is an interesting range of hors d'oeuvres ideas. Select from them using color, taste, and texture as your guides. This is the time to use the chafing dish and the warming tray gifts, and any other lovely trays and platters you own. Showmanship is as important in your home as on a stage, for the presentation of food is a revealing showcase of your sense of taste.

DEVILED HAM DIP

To make 1½ cups of dip
1 *cup dairy sour cream*
1 *(4½-ounce) can deviled ham*
½ *package dehydrated onion soup mix*

Stir deviled ham and onion soup mix into sour cream. Mix well. Chill. Serve as a dip with potato chips or crackers.

SHRIMP DIP

To make about 2 cups of dip
1 *cup dairy sour cream*
1 *(3-ounce) package cream cheese*
½ *cup chopped olives*
1 *tablespoon white horseradish*
½ *teaspoon sugar*
¼ *teaspoon Worcestershire sauce*

157

Combine sour cream and cream cheese until smooth. Add chopped olives, horseradish, sugar, and Worcestershire sauce. Refrigerate until ready to serve. Serve as a dip for cooked cold shrimp.

SOUR CREAM–CAVIAR DIP

To make 1½ cups of dip
½ *pint dairy sour cream*
1 *(3-ounce) package chive cream cheese*
¼ *cup red caviar*
¼ *teaspoon Worcestershire sauce*

Mash sour cream and chive cream cheese together, until well blended and fluffy. Gently add red caviar (being careful not to mash it) and Worcestershire sauce. Chill until ready to serve as a dip with potato chips or crackers.

SCAMPI

To serve 6 to 8
¼ *cup olive oil*
2 *cloves garlic, minced*
1 *pound shrimp, shelled and cleaned*
¼ *cup dried parsley flakes*

Heat olive oil in a large skillet. Add minced garlic and brown lightly. Add shrimp and sauté until bright pink, about 4 minutes. Sprinkle parsley flakes over all, and mix well. Serve hot, with toothpicks or fancy spears.

RUMAKI

To make 2 dozen
8 *slices bacon, cut in thirds*
6 *chicken livers, quartered*
8 *water chestnuts, cut in thirds*
¼ *cup soy sauce*
2 *tablespoons brown sugar*

Wrap a piece of bacon around a chicken liver piece and a slice of water chestnut. Spear with a wooden toothpick. Combine soy sauce and brown sugar in a small plastic bag. Place speared bits in the bag and seal shut with a wired closure. Marinate for several hours. Shift the position of the bag frequently so that the marinade is evenly distributed. Drain speared bits when ready to cook, and broil in a pan for 2 minutes, then turn and broil 3 minutes more, or until bacon is crisp. Serve at once.

CHOPPED CHICKEN LIVERS

To make 1 cup
1 *large onion, sliced thin*
2 *tablespoons chicken fat or butter*
½ *pound chicken livers*
1 *shelled hard-cooked egg*
¼ *teaspoon salt*
⅛ *teaspoon pepper*

Sauté sliced onion in chicken fat until golden. Push onions to side of pan and add chicken livers; brown livers, turning them so that every side will be seared. Empty the skillet, including the remaining rendered fat, into a chopping bowl. Add the hard-cooked egg, salt, and pepper. Chop very fine. Chill. Serve as spread with crackers.

CHOPPED HERRING

A QUICK-TRICK WAY

To make 1 cup
1 *(12-ounce) jar herring in wine sauce, drained*
½ *apple, cored and peeled*
Salt and pepper (optional)

Empty herring into a chopping bowl. Add cut-up apple. Chop very fine. Add salt and pepper to taste if desired. Serve as spread with crackers.

159

ASPARAGUS–CHEESE DANISH

A QUICK-TRICK WAY

To make 12 appetizers
12 *slices thin-sliced white bread*
¼ *cup cheddar cheese spread*
12 *canned asparagus spears*
2 *tablespoons melted butter*

Trim the crusts from the bread slices. Spread each slice with soft cheddar cheese spread. Lay an asparagus spear diagonally across the slice. Fold the two free corners of the slice toward the middle and fasten with a toothpick. Brush the exposed top of the bread with melted butter. Place on a buttered baking pan and bake for 10 minutes in a 350-degree oven, or until cheese is melted and bread is slightly toasted. Remove and serve at once.

CHEESE BALLS

To make 1 dozen 1-inch balls	*To make 2 dozen 1-inch balls*
½ *ounce brandy*	1 *ounce brandy*
½ *pound ricotta cheese*	1 *pound ricotta cheese*
1 *egg, beaten*	2 *eggs, beaten*
⅛ *teaspoon salt*	¼ *teaspoon salt*
¼ *cup flour*	½ *cup flour*
2 *cups cooking oil*	2 *cups cooking oil*
Confectioners' sugar	*Confectioners' sugar*

Mix the brandy into the cheese with a fork. Add beaten egg. Add salt and flour, mixing thoroughly. Refrigerate dough for 1 hour. Heat oil in a small, deep saucepan. Using 2 teaspoons, scooping with 1 and pushing off with the other, drop mixture into the hot oil by the teaspoonful. Do a few balls at a time; watch them brown and bob up to the surface, then remove the browned balls with a slotted spoon and drain them on paper towels.* Cool slightly and sprinkle with powdered confectioners' sugar. May be made early in the day; do not sprinkle with sugar. To reheat, bake in a 350-degree oven for 15 minutes, then sprinkle with sugar.

* Do not discard oil; pour through a strainer and store for reuse.

QUICHE LORRAINE

To serve 4 to 6
1 *(1-crust) Cream Cheese Pie Pastry, unbaked (see page 140)**
⅔ *cup Swiss cheese*
1 *small onion*
4 *bacon strips, fried and drained*
2 *eggs, beaten*
⅔ *cup dairy sour cream*
½ *teaspoon salt*
½ *teaspoon Worcestershire sauce*

In a chopping bowl, combine Swiss cheese, onion, and cooked bacon and chop into a coarse mixture. Fill the bottom of the pastry shell with this mixture. In a separate bowl, combine beaten eggs, sour cream, salt, and Worcestershire sauce. Pour over the cheese–bacon mixture. Bake pie in a 375-degree oven for about 20 minutes. The prepared recipe can be baked beforehand and reheated, or refrigerated and baked just before serving.

MUSHROOMS STUFFED WITH CRAB MEAT

To make 2 dozen appetizers
24 *fresh mushrooms, 1½-inch diameter*
1 *(4-ounce) can crab meat, chopped*
1 *(3-ounce) package chive cream cheese*
½ *teaspoon Worcestershire sauce*

Remove stems from mushrooms and reserve. Wash mushrooms well and dry. Trim stems, wash, dry, and chop fine. Add chopped crab meat to chopped mushroom stems. Mash in chive cream cheese. Add Worcestershire sauce. Fill mushroom cavities with this mixture. Place on a broiling tray, filling side up. Broil for 10 minutes, or until mushroom caps are cooked through. Serve hot.

---

* The unbaked pastry shell may be prepared from a mix or bought at the frozen food counter at your grocery.

PIGS IN A BLANKET

A QUICK-TRICK WAY

To make 20 appetizers
1 *package (10 biscuits) refrigerated biscuits*
20 *cocktail-sized frankfurters*
¼ *cup apricot preserves*
2 *teaspoons prepared mustard*

Separate biscuits; cut each in half. Roll each piece of biscuit flat, place a frankfurter in the middle, and seal dough closed all around it. Bake in a 400-degree oven for 10 to 15 minutes, until dough is golden brown. Combine apricot preserves and mustard into a sauce. Serve sauce in the center of a tray of hot frankfurter appetizers. Have toothpicks available for easy handling and dipping.

PIZZA PLEASERS

A QUICK-TRICK WAY

To make 10 to 12 individual pizzas
1 *package (10 to 12 biscuits) refrigerated biscuits*
1 *(8-ounce) can tomato sauce with onions*
¼ *teaspoon oregano*
½ *cup mozzarella cheese, diced small*
2 *tablespoons Parmesan cheese*

Separate biscuits; on a lightly floured surface flatten each biscuit to ⅛-inch thickness. Place on an ungreased baking sheet. Spread each biscuit with sauce; sprinkle with oregano. Top with a sprinkling of mozzarella cheese, and then Parmesan cheese. Bake in a 400-degree oven for 10 to 15 minutes, until biscuits are golden and cheese is melted. Serve at once.

PIZZA CRESCENTS

A QUICK-TRICK WAY

To make 16 crescents
2 *packages refrigerated crescent rolls*
¾ *cup diced cooked ham*

¾ cup diced salami

½ cup diced mozzarella cheese

1 (8-ounce) can tomato sauce with onions

½ teaspoon oregano

Separate rolls and carefully unroll each. In a small bowl, combine the ham, salami, cheese, sauce, and oregano. Spoon mixture onto the center of each roll. Reroll each crescent, starting at the widest end. Place on greased baking sheet. Bake at 375 degrees for 12 to 15 minutes or until golden brown. Serve hot.

EGGS À LA RUSSE

A QUICK-TRICK WAY

To serve 4

4 shelled hard-cooked eggs

½ cup mayonnaise

½ cup chili sauce

2 teaspoons capers

Paprika

Split hard-cooked eggs in half lengthwise. Arrange 2 halves on each plate. Stir mayonnaise and chili sauce together. Spoon over the eggs, letting some of the egg show. Garnish with capers. Sprinkle with a dash of paprika. Serve cold.

SUPER DEVILED EGGS

To serve 12

6 shelled hard-cooked eggs, halved lengthwise

1 tablespoon stuffed olives, finely chopped

2 tablespoons mayonnaise

1 teaspoon prepared mustard

⅛ teaspoon salt

Dash of pepper

Paprika

Parsley

Scoop egg yolks carefully out of their sockets and place in a bowl. Mash together. Add finely chopped olives, mayonnaise, mustard, salt, and pepper; blend all thoroughly. Refill the egg white sockets with this mixture, swirling the tops decoratively. Sprinkle with paprika and garnish platter with fresh parsley. Refrigerate until serving time.

❧19❧

Freezer Facts

IF THERE IS NOT A FREEZER IN YOUR HOME, NOR THE PROSPECT OF one in the immediate future, I can only hope that one day there will be. A freezer is probably the most useful yet the most misunderstood, underused appliance in the home. For those of you who own a freezer but who have not yet discovered the wonderful world of freezing, I can only encourage you to be adventurous, and to find ways to make your freezer pay its way by saving you both time and money.

Whether you are blessed with a freezer or only have a freezing compartment in your refrigerator, the most important thing to remember is to cook an extra meal especially for the freezer when you are preparing dinner. With very little extra effort you will have a second meal in the bank.

Your freezer will not improve the flavor or the quality of anything you put into it; it will merely hold food safely until you want to use it. Be sure that you freeze top-quality foods for best results. I have included a chart at the end of this chapter which lists the length of time different categories of foods may be safely stored in the freezer. This chart is based on keeping the freezer at zero degrees Fahrenheit. Simply keeping foods frozen is not sufficient protection. The higher the storage temperature rises above zero, the greater the growth of bacteria. Since practically all bacterial growth ceases at zero degrees Fahrenheit, it is most important to maintain this constant temperature.

Successful freezing also depends on your ability to wrap foods properly. Improperly wrapped frozen foods lose their moisture, flavor, and tenderness, and are prone to a condition known as "freezer burn." To prevent this from happening, use moisture-proof and vaporproof materials. Ordinary waxed paper, butcher paper, or cellophane are not sufficient. Use special containers that are especially usable for the freezer, such as plastic, waxed cartons, and aluminum foil containers. Glass jars may be used, but they become brittle when very cold. Special care must be taken not to shatter them accidentally. Aluminum foil, heavy freezer paper, and heavy plastic bags are excellent. All must be sealed airtight with tape or wired closures. Air space inside the packages tends to rob frozen food of its moisture during storage.

Cooked meat and prepared dinners are best frozen in their own gravy, even if you have to water down the gravy to provide enough to submerge the cooked food in it.

Containers should be filled to one-half inch to one and a half inches from the top, depending on the moisture contained in the food. Juices and soups have a high moisture content and will need the most expansion room when freezing.

Almost every type of food can be frozen successfully. The trick is to find out the form in which it freezes best. For instance, eggs cannot be frozen in their shells—they would burst; but you can remove the eggs from the shells, stir them together, and make egg cubes in your ice cube tray equal to the number of eggs you have used. This technique would be a saving for someone who had a sudden avalanche of eggs on hand and no way of using them up fast enough. The ice cube technique is good for making "soup cubes" out of leftover chicken soup. Once the cubes are set, they may be removed from the tray and placed in a container in the freezer. When you want to add bouillon to a canned soup, just reach in for a couple of soup cubes.

The general rule for freezing and refreezing is that an item is entitled to one trip to the freezer in each condition—once uncooked, once cooked. This means that you may take a roast out of the freezer, cook it, and return it to the freezer to be used as leftovers. Once you heat it again, finish it, since it may not be returned for additional freezer time.

To thaw or not to thaw before cooking can be a puzzling

question. Fruits should always be thawed in their original containers and opened only at the moment of serving. Vegetables need not be thawed; they can be dropped directly into boiling water when frozen. Meats do not have to be thawed before cooking; just increase the cooking time to account for the meat's frozen state. Once thawed, use frozen food promptly.

Cakes, pies, and bread all freeze well. Homemade cakes freeze better if they are unfrosted; leave the frosting job for the day you serve it. Pies may be frozen baked or unbaked, but fruit pies seem to be better when they are frozen unbaked, and then placed in the oven while still frozen. The trip to the freezer seems to give the dough a flakier crust, too. Freeze sliced breads and remove the slices a few hours before using them. You can make a real saving on breadstuffs and have absolutely fresh bread of any kind at your fingertips. If you are planning toasted sandwiches, pop the frozen bread into the toaster with no time for thawing.

What doesn't freeze well? Cooked whites of eggs become rubbery, boiled potatoes become soggy, and custard-type pies are generally not retrieved in satisfactory condition. Salad greens, whole tomatoes, and vegetables which will not be cooked after freezing should not be frozen at all. Mayonnaise dressing will separate, unless it is mixed with other food. And some cheeses, like cottage cheese, cheddar cheese, and cream cheese, tend to change in consistency, while other types of cheese freeze quite well.

Why bother with a freezer when the grocery store is near enough for daily trips? Because those daily trips will cost you a great deal of time, energy, and excess money. I know that you understand how one trip a week to the grocer will save time and energy. But money? How? As you probably know or will soon find out, the prices of meat and poultry, the most expensive items in your food budget, fluctuate from week to week. If you have a freezer and learn to use it wisely, you will discover that a great saving can be made when you stockpile meat and poultry at their lowest prices.

Instead of buying a variety of different meats each week, you will be able to invest your meat money in the one or two items that are an especially good buy. If you buy in quantity, you can almost be assured of being able to wait until a particular item is offered on special sale again. Thus, you can arrange to have in the freezer, at its lowest price, every meat and poultry item you use regularly. While the market may fluctuate, you are dining merrily at the lowest price per item. Food represents a major expense in your budget, so it is good business sense to explore the ways in which you can save money without sacrificing quality.

I urge you, however, not to get involved in a freezer plan whereby you supposedly get your freezer almost free while you purchase your food in bulk from a home delivery service. Although the sales pitch sounds good, this plan is often an expensive and disappointing lesson since you do not have absolute control in selecting each item. I also do not advocate plans for purchasing whole hindquarters and forequarters of meat. You would not normally buy many of the cuts in this quarter if you had the choice; and many times you are left with meat meals that are not satisfactory. Also, while the price may sound attractive, you must do a little arithmetic to find out what the real price is: count on at least 30 percent waste from fat, bones, and trimming, and add that on to the "bargain" price for a quarter of beef. You would do better to choose exactly the cuts of meat you want and buy them at their lowest prices during each two- or three-month period. In this way you will enjoy every meal and save money at the same time.

When selecting prepackaged frozen foods, be sure that the package has not been above the safety line in your grocer's freezer cabinet. Dig down, and get the solid packages from the bottom. Then you'll be certain that the package was not thawing and refreezing as it was shifted around by other shoppers. Don't buy any packages that seem to be softened. Check to see that the thermometer in the store's frozen food case reads zero degrees or less.

If you have a long marketing list, buy the frozen food last to shorten the time it spends between freezers. Avoid torn or dirty looking packages. And do not buy more of each item than you will use within a safe storage period.

There is definitely money and time to be saved by having a freezer. Investigate this field of food management in greater depth to see how it may be advantageous for you. It is a major way to beat the high cost of food!

RECOMMENDED STORAGE PERIODS FOR FROZEN FOODS

PRODUCT	MONTHS
Fruits	12
Vegetables	12
Beef	10 to 12
Veal	10 to 12
Lamb	10 to 12
Pork	4 to 6
Poultry	6 to 8
Fatty fish	3
Lean fish	6
Shellfish	6 to 8
Ground beef	6 to 8
Sausage	1 to 3
Cheese	3 to 4
Cream	4 to 6
Eggs	6 to 8
Bread, baked	12
Bread, unbaked	½ to 2
Cakes, baked	4 to 8
Cakes, unbaked	2 to 3
Pies	2 to 6
Cookies, baked	12
Cookies, unbaked	6 to 9
Sandwiches	½ to 3
Cooked meats	3 to 8

20

The Last Word

HAVE YOU EVER HEARD OF A MOTHER WHO DIDN'T WANT TO HAVE the last word? It's a prerogative that comes with experience, maturity, and a sneaking suspicion that something important may have been left unsaid.

My objective was to help you over a few difficult cooking hurdles and, at the same time, to give you a philosophy to enable you to jump over future ones on your own. I could not conceive of writing a simple beginner's cookbook, and so I have proceeded to write as I would teach you to swim: throw you in the water and hope you won't drown before learning! I hope I have strung out many life preservers along the way, and that I may play some small part in helping you to develop a sense of self-confidence in the kitchen. At times, in discussing your attitudes in the kitchen, I have been referring to other rooms as well, for I feel that all your attitudes are interrelated. I would like to see you beat the statistics of failing marriages with old-fashioned womanly prowess. An innate sense of homemaking never goes out of style!

Lastly, I presume that if you take good care of your mother-in-law's son, he will cherish you and take good care of you in return. And so I have devised for you a special recipe called Marriage Stew. I hope you will be able to enjoy a hearty helping every day of your married life!

MARRIAGE STEW

Take: 2 hearts full of love
Add: 1 quart of communication
1 measure of respect
1 jigger of loyalty
1 cup of appreciation
1 pint of friendship

Simmer together until both hearts are well coated with mixture.

Then blend in: 1 tablespoon sweet talk
1 tablespoon spicy differences

Sprinkle with: Essence of justice
Essence of humor

If the sauce sours after standing, reappraise the ingredients to see if anything was accidentally omitted. Add at once. Taste occasionally for sweetness. The sauce should be both sweet and tangy; it should have piquancy and yet be smooth. If an occasional lump appears, blend it out immediately before it spoils the stew. Hearts should be served touching each other, each holding its own shape, yet creating a double form. Once you have the recipe down pat, the rest is all gravy!

Menus

BRUNCH

Tomato Juice with Wedges of Lime
Applesauce Pancakes*
Zesty Scrambled Eggs*
Crisp Bacon
Hard Rolls
Sour Cream Coffee Cake*
Coffee or Tea

Orange Juice in Old Fashioned Glasses
with Pineapple Ring and Cherry
Eggs Benedict*
Mushrooms Stuffed with Crab Meat*
Baked Apple Ambrosia*
Orange–Nut Bread*
Coffee or Tea

*Recipe in this book.

172

LUNCHEON FOR THE GIRLS

Melon Balls Chilled in Ginger Ale,
Garnished with Mint
*Cannelloni au Gratin**
Tossed Green Salad, Oil–Vinegar Dressing
Italian Bread Sticks
*Apple Pie**
Coffee or Tea

*Gazpacho**
*Scallop Kabobs**
*Mushroom Crepes**
Tossed Green Salad, Oil–Vinegar Dressing
Small Rolls
Lemon Sherbet
*Chocolate Brownies**
Coffee or Tea

V.I.P. DINNER

*Eggs à la Russe**
*Chicken Breasts in White Wine Sauce**
*Green Noodles in Spinach Sauce**
*Elegant Carrots**
Tossed Green Salad, Oil–Vinegar Dressing
Blueberry Muffins
or French Bread
*Hot Fruit Compote**
Coconut Macaroons or Cookies*
Coffee or Tea

*Recipe in this book.

Hot Crab Meat on Herbed Croutons*
Sliced Steak with Burgundy–Mushroom Gravy*
Wild and White Rice
Green Beans Amandine*
Tossed Green Salad, Oil–Vinegar Dressing
Corn Muffins
or Italian Bread
Blueberry Parfaits
(using blueberry pie filling as directed in Chapter 3)
Coffee or Tea

Quiche Lorraine*
Roast Duckling with Orange–Brandy Sauce*
Praline Yams*
Carrots Veronique*
Tossed Green Salad, Oil–Vinegar Dressing
Apricot–Orange Nut Loaf*
or French Bread
Ice Cream Bombe with Strawberry Sauce*
Coffee or Tea

Antipasto Tray
(salami, thinly sliced; pickled beets; pickled herring;
olives; anchovies; artichoke hearts; pimiento strips;
tuna fish, in large chunks)
Veal Scaloppine*
Fettucini Alfredo*
Zucchini and Tomatoes*
Lettuce and Raw Spinach Salad, Oil–Vinegar Dressing
Onion Crescents*
or Italian Bread with Sesame Seeds
Torte Angelique*
Coffee or Tea

*Recipe in this book.

174

BUFFET

Shrimp Creole* in Chafing Dish
Rice Ring
(as prepared in recipe for Mushroom Sauce on Rice Ring*)
Cherry-Glazed Turkey Roll,* sliced
Mandarin Sherbet Mold*
Cole Slaw
Orange–Nut Muffins*
or Tiny Seeded Rolls
Apple Strudel*
Coffee or Tea

Beef Stroganoff*
Wild and White Rice
Island Fried Shrimp*
Pineapple–Cucumber Mold*
Sesame Bread Sticks
Cheese Cake,* Strawberry Glaze*
Coffee or Tea

Meat Balls* in Chafing Dish
Crab Meat Tetrazzini*
Cole Slaw Gelatin Ring*
Buttered Carrots and Peas
Hot Buttered Italian Bread
(with garlic if desired)
Orange Sponge Cake,* Lemon-Custard Cake Sauce*
Coffee or Tea

*Recipe in this book.

Shrimp Newburg*
Browned Rice
Chicken in Pineapple Sauce*
Waldorf Salad Mold*
Green Beans Gourmet*
Hush Puppies*
Pecan Pie*
Coffee or Tea

SUNDAY FAMILY DINNER

Clam Bisque*
Sauerbraten*
Lemon-Buttered Cabbage*
Parsleyed Potatoes*
Beet Salad Jell*
Herbed Butter Crescents*
Mocha Refrigerator Cake*
Coffee or Tea

Fresh Fruit Salad
(orange segments; apple chunks;
banana slices; fresh whole strawberries)
Roast Turkey*
Sweet Potato Casserole*
Creamed Spinach*
Tossed Green Salad, Homemade French Dressing*
Onion–Rye Muffins*
Pots de Crème*
Lemon Wafers*
Coffee or Tea

*Recipe in this book.

Index

179

Sour Cream
  -Caviar Dip, 158
  Coffee Cake, 145–46
Spaghetti
  Crab Meat Tetrazzini, 116
  Milanese, 114–15
  with Tomato-Meat Sauce, 115
  with White Clam Sauce, 114
Spices, 25–31
Spinach
  Creamed, 108
  Green Noodles in Spinach
    Sauce, 113–14
Sponge Cake, Orange, 144–45
Staples
  for desserts, 139
  for entertaining, 13–17
Steak
  Beef Stroganoff, 78–79
  Burgundy-Mushroom Gravy
    for, 132
  Carving, 72
  London Broil, 76
  Sliced, with Burgundy-
    Mushroom Gravy, 76
Stock, Soup, 41
Storing
  Chicken, 88
  Frozen foods, 169
  Meat, precautions for, 59–60
  Stuffing, 88–89
  Vegetables, 97–101
Strawberry Glaze, 145
Strudel, Apple, 143–44
Stuffing, 95
  Storing leftover, 88–89
Sweet Potato Casserole, 107

T

Terms, cooking, definition of, 18–
  22
Tomatoes
  Aspic, 127
  -Rice Soup, 42
  Spicy Stewed, 109
  Zucchini and, 110
Turkey
  Cherry-Glazed Turkey Roll, 95
  Roast, 94–95
  Roasting guide, 89

U

Utensils
  for carving, 60
  for kitchen, 11–13, 17

V

Veal
  Carving, 72
  Chops in Mushroom Sauce, 83
  Cutlet Cordon Bleu, 82–83
  Cuts of, 64–65
  Oriental Roast, 84
  Scaloppine, 82
  Storage of frozen, 169
Vegetables
  Buying and storing, 97–101
  Cabbage, Lemon-Buttered, 103
  Cauliflower, French Fried, 104
  Cooking hints, 101–02
  for soups, 40–41
  Freezing hints, 167, 169
  Hollandaise Sauce for, 134–35
  Liquid of, in soups, 40
  Mushroom Sauce on Rice Ring,
    104–05
  Onion Rings, French Fried, 105
  Salad Mold, 126
  Spices for, 28–30
  Spinach, Creamed, 108
  Tomatoes, Spicy Stewed, 109
  Velouté Sauce for, 133
  White Sauce for, 134–35
  See also specific types
Vichyssoise, 46

W

Waldorf Salad Mold, 123
Weights and measures, 22–24
  Individual meat portions, 59
White Sauce, 134
Wild Rice and Chicken Salad
  Mold, 128–29

Y

Yams, Praline, 108

Z

Zucchini, 109
  and Tomatoes, 110

182